PAPER
BACK
LYRICS

COMPLETE
OVER 17

The

1970s

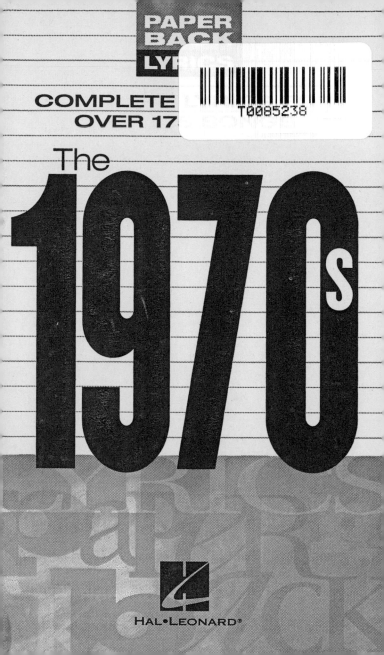

HAL•LEONARD®

ISBN 13: 978-1-4234-1194-9
ISBN 10: 1-4234-1194-3

HAL•LEONARD®
CORPORATION

7777 W. BLUEMOUND RD. P.O. BOX 13819 MILWAUKEE, WI 53213

Visit Hal Leonard Online at
www.halleonard.com

CONTENTS

5

After the Love Has Gone

Words and Music by David Foster, Jay Graydon and Bill Champlin

recorded by Earth, Wind & Fire

For a while to love was all we could do;
We were young and we knew,
And our eyes were alive.
Deep inside we knew our love was true.
For awhile we paid no mind to the past,
We knew love would last.
Every night
Somethin' right
Would invite us to begin the dance.

Somethin' happened along the way;
What used to be happy was sad.
Somethin' happened along the way
And yesterday was all we had.

Oh, after the love has gone,
How could you lead me on,
And not let me stay around?
Oh, after the love has gone,
What used to be right is wrong.
Can love that's lost be found?

For awhile,
To love each other was all we would ever need.
Love was strong for so long,
Never knew that what was wrong,
Baby, wasn't right.
We tried to find what we had
'Til sadness was all we shared.
We were scared this affair
Would lead our love into…

Somethin' happened along the way;
Yesterday was all we had.
Somethin' happened along the way;
What used to be happy is sad.
Somethin' happened along the way;
What used to be was all we had.
Oh, after the love has gone,
How could you lead me on
And not let me stay around?

Oh, after the love has gone,
What used to be right is wrong.
Can love that's lost be found?
Oh, after the love has gone,
What used to be right is wrong.
Can love that's lost be found?

After the Lovin'

Words and Music by Alan Bernstein and Richie Adams

recorded by Engelbert Humperdinck

So, I sing you to sleep, after the lovin',
With a song I just wrote yesterday.
And I hope you can hear what the words
And the music have to say.

It's so hard to explain ev'rything that I'm feelin'.
Face to face, I just seem to go dry.
But I love you so much,
That the sound of your voice can get me high.
Thanks for takin' me on a one way trip to the sun.
And thanks for turnin' me into a someone.

Twice:
So, I sing you to sleep, after the lovin'.
I brush back the hair from your eyes.
And the love on your face is so real
That it makes me wanna cry.
And I know that my song
Isn't sayin' anything new.
Oh, but after the lovin',
I'm still in love with you.

Yes, after the lovin',
I'm still in love with you.
Mm, after the lovin',
I'm still in love with you.

Ain't No Way to Treat a Lady

Words and Music by Harriet Schock

recorded by Helen Reddy

I guess it was yourself you were involved with.
I would've sworn it was me.
I might've found out sooner,
If you'd only let me close enough to see.

Refrain:
That ain't no way to treat a lady,
No way to treat your baby, your woman, your friend.
That ain't no way to treat a lady, no way,
But maybe it's a way for us to end.

I was only bein' a picture
With all the colors I know,
While you were busy lookin'
Into wide blue mirrors and lovin' the show.

Refrain

There's a funny kind of consolation keepin' me sane.
And I'd really like to share it, crawl on deep in my brain,
And see the times you never felt me lovin' you or needin' you.
So leavin' you now, you still won't know how to feel the pain.

I was lookin' out for my happiness
While you were lookin' within.
And before you know your own reflection
Always starts to tire you, it had happened again.

Refrain

Afternoon Delight

Words and Music by Bill Danoff

recorded by Starland Vocal Band

Gonna find my baby, gonna hold her tight,
Gonna grab some afternoon delight.
My motto's always been "When it's right, it's right,"
Why wait until the middle of a cold, dark night.
When ev'rything's a little clearer in the light of day,
And we know the night is always gonna be here anyway?

Thinking of you's working up my appetite,
Looking forward to a little afternoon delight.
Rubbing sticks and stones together make the sparks ignite
And the thought of rubbing you is getting so exciting.
Sky rockets in flight, afternoon delight,
Afternoon delight, afternoon delight.

Started out this morning feeling so polite,
I always thought a fish could not be caught who didn't bite.
But you got some bait a-waiting and I think I might
Like nibbling a little afternoon delight.
Sky rockets in flight, afternoon delight,
Afternoon delight, afternoon delight.

Be waiting for me, baby, when I come around.
We can make a lot of loving 'fore the sun gone down.

Thinking of you's working up my appetite,
Looking forward to a little afternoon delight.
Rubbing sticks and stones together make the sparks ignite
And the thought of rubbing you is getting so exciting.
Sky rockets in flight, afternoon delight,
Afternoon delight, afternoon delight.

Afternoon delight, afternoon delight.

Ain't No Mountain High Enough

Words and Music by Nickolas Ashford and Valerie Simpson

recorded by Diana Ross

Now, if you need me, call me.
No matter where you are,
No matter how far.
Don't worry baby.
Just call out my name.
I'll be there in a hurry.
You don't have to worry,
'Cause baby there

Refrain:
Ain't no mountain high enough,
Ain't no valley low enough,
Ain't no river wide enough
To keep me from getting to you, babe.

Remember the day I set you free?
I told you could always count on me.
And from that day on,
I made a vow:
I'll be there when you want me,
Some way somehow.
'Cause baby there

Refrain

And no wind,
And no rain or winter's cold
Can stop me, baby.
Oh baby, if you are my goal.
(If you're ever in trouble,
I'll be there on the double.
Just send for me baby!
Oh, baby!)

My love is alive,
Deep down in my heart,
Although we are miles apart.
If you ever need a helping hand,
I'll be there on the double,
Just as fast as I can.
Don't you know that there

Refrain Three Times

Twice:
Ain't no mountain high enough,
Ain't no valley low enough,
Ain't no river wide enough
To keep me from you.

Twice:
Ah.
Nothing can keep me,
Keep me from you.
Ain't no mountain high enough.
Nothing can keep me,
Keep me from you.

The Air That I Breathe

Words and Music by Albert Hammond and Michael Hazelwood

recorded by The Hollies

If I could make a wish I think I'd pass,
Can't think of anything I need.
No cigarettes, no sleep, no light, no sound,
Nothing to eat, no books to read.

Making love with you
Has left me peaceful, warm and tired.
What more could I ask,
There's nothing left to be desired.

Peace came upon me and it leaves me weak.
Sleep, silent angel, go to sleep.

Sometimes,
All I need is the air that I breathe.
And to love you,
All I need is the air that I breathe.
Yes, to love you,
All I need is the air that I breathe.

Peace came upon me and it leaves me weak.
Sleep, silent angel, go to sleep.

All by Myself

Music by Sergei Rachmaninoff
Words and Additional Music by Eric Carmen

recorded by Eric Carmen

When I was young, I never needed anyone,
And making love was just for fun.
Those days are gone.

Livin' alone, I think of all the friends I've known.
But when I dial the telephone,
Nobody's home.

Refrain:
All by myself,
Don't wanna be all by myself anymore.

Hard to be sure. Sometimes I feel so insecure,
And loves so distant and obscure
Remains the cure.

Refrain Twice

When I was young, I never needed anyone,
And making love was just for fun.
Those days are gone.

Refrain

Alone Again Naturally

Words and Music by Raymond O'Sullivan

recorded by Gilbert O'Sullivan

Oh, in a little while from now, if I'm not feeling any less sour
I promise myself to treat myself and visit a nearby tower.
And climbing to the top will throw myself off
In an effort to make it clear to whoever what it's like
    when you're shattered,
Left standing in the lurch at a church where people saying,
"My God that's tough, she's stood him up, no point in us remaining.
    We may as well go home."
As I did on my own; alone again, naturally.

To think that only yesterday, I was cheerful, bright and gay;
Looking forward to, well, who wouldn't do the role
    I was about to play:
But as if to knock me down, reality came around;
And without so much, as a mere touch, cut me into little pieces:
Leaving me to doubt talk about God in his mercy,
Who if he really does exist why did he desert me in my hour of need?
I truly am indeed alone again, naturally.

It seems to me that there are more hearts
Broken in the world that can't be mended,
Left unattended: what do we do?
What do we do?

Now looking back over the years, and whatever else that appears;
I remember I cried, when my father died, never wishing to
   hide the tears:
And at sixty-five years old, my mother, God rest her soul,
Couldn't understand why the only man she had ever loved had been
   taken:
Leaving her to start with a heart so badly broken,
Despite encouragement from me no words were ever spoken:
And when she passed away I cried and cried all day:
Alone again, naturally. Alone again, naturally.

American Pie

Words and Music by Don McLean

recorded by Don McLean

A long, long time ago
I can still remember
How that music used to make me smile.
And I knew if I had my chance
That I could make those people dance
And maybe they'd be happy for a while.
But February made me shiver
With ev'ry paper I'd deliver.
Bad news on the doorstep
I couldn't take one more step.
I can't remember if I cried
When I read about his widowed bride.
Something touched me deep inside
The day the music died. So

Refrain:
Bye-bye Miss American Pie
Drove my Chevy to the levee but the levee was dry.
Them good old boys were drinkin' whiskey and rye,
Singin' this'll be the day that I die.
This'll be the day that I die.

Did you write the book of love
And do you have faith in God above?
If the Bible tells you so.
Now do you believe in rock and roll?
Can music save your mortal soul
And can you teach me how to dance real slow?
Well, I know that you're in love with him
'Cause I saw you dancin' in the gym.
You both kicked off your shoes.
Man, I dig those rhythm and blues.
I was a lonely teenage broncin' buck
With a pink carnation and a pick-up truck.
But I knew I was out of luck
The day the music died.
I started singing

Refrain

Now for ten years we've been on our own,
And moss grows fat on a rollin' stone
But that's not how it used to be
When the jester sang for the king and queen
In a coat he borrowed from James Dean
And a voice that came from you and me
Oh and while the king was looking down,
The jester stole his thorny crown
The courtroom was adjourned,
No verdict was returned
And while Lenin read a book on Marx
The quartet practiced in the park
And we sang dirges in the dark
The day the music died
We were singin'

Refrain

Helter-skelter in the summer swelter
The birds flew off with a fallout shelter
Eight miles high and fallin' fast,
It landed foul on the grass
The players tried for a forward pass,
With the jester on the sidelines in a cast
Now the half-time air was sweet perfume
While the sergeants played a marching tune
We all got up to dance
But we never got the chance
'Cause the players tried to take the field,
The marching band refused to yield
Do you recall what was revealed
The day the music died
We started singin'

Refrain

And there we were all in one place,
A generation lost in space
With no time left to start again
So come on, Jack be nimble, Jack be quick,
Jack Flash sat on a candlestick
'Cause fire is the devil's only friend
And as I watched him on the stage
My hands were clenched in fits of rage
No angel born in hell
Could break that Satan's spell
And as the flames climbed high into the night
To light the sacrificial rite
I saw Satan laughing with delight
The day the music died
He was singin'

I met a girl who sang the blues
And I asked her for some happy news,
But she just smiled and turned away.
I went down to the sacred store
Where I heard the music years before,
But the man there said the music wouldn't play.
And in the streets the children screamed,
The lovers cried and the poets dreamed.
But not a word was spoken, the church bells all were broken.
And the three men I admire most,
The Father, Son and the Holy Ghost,
They caught the last train for the coast
The day the music died.
And they were singin'

Refrain

An American Trilogy

Words and Music by Mickey Newbury

recorded by Mickey Newbury, Elvis Presley

How I wish I was in the land of cotton,
Old things they are not forgotten,
Look away, look away, look away Dixieland.
Oh, I wish I was in Dixie, away, away,
In Dixieland I take my stand
To live and die in Dixie.
'Cause Dixieland, that's where I was born
Early, Lord, one frosty morning,
Look away, look away, look away Dixieland.

Glory, glory hallelujah,
Glory, glory hallelujah,
Glory, glory hallelujah,
His truth is marching on.

So hush, little children, don't you cry,
You know your daddy's bound to die.
But all my trials, Lord, soon be over.

And I Love You So

Words and Music by Don McLean

recorded by Bobby Goldsboro, Perry Como

And I love you so, the people ask me how,
How I've lived till now; I tell them I don't know.
I guess they understand how lonely life has been,
But life began again, the day you took my hand.

Refrain:
And yes, I know how lonely [loveless] life can be,
The shadows follow me and the night won't set me free.
But I don't let the evening get [bring] me down,
Now that you're around me.

And you love me too; your thoughts are just for me.
You set my spirit free; I'm happy that you do.
The book of life is brief, and once a page is read,
All but love is dead, that is my belief.

Refrain

And I love you so, the people ask me how,
How I've lived till now;
I tell them I don't know.

American Woman

Written by Burton Cummings, Randy Bachman, Gary Peterson and Jim Kale

recorded by The Guess Who

American woman, gonna mess your mind.
American woman, she gonna mess your mind.
American woman, gonna mess your mind.
American woman, gonna mess your mind.

I say A, I say M, I say E, I say R, say I, use C, say A, N.
American woman, gonna mess your mind.
American woman, gonna mess your mind.
American woman, gonna mess your mind.

Refrain 1 (Twice):
American woman, stay away from me,
American woman, mama let me be.
Don't come hangin' around my door,
I don't wanna see your face no more,
I got more important things to do
Than spend my time growin' old with you.
Now woman, I said stay away,
American woman, listen what I say.

Refrain 2:
American Woman, stay away from me,
American woman, mama let me be.
Don't come hangin' around my door,
I don't wanna see your face no more,
I got more important things to do
Than spend my time growin', old with you.
Now woman, I said stay away,
American woman, mama let me be.

Go, gotta get away, gotta get away, now go, go, go.
I'm gonna leave you, woman, gonna leave you woman,
Bye, bye. Bye, bye. Bye, bye. Bye, bye.

You're no good for me, I'm no good for you.
Gonna look you right in the eye, tell you what I'm gonna do.
You know I'm gonna leave, you know I'm gonna go.
You know I'm gonna leave, you know I'm gonna go, woman.
I'm gonna leave, woman, goodbye, American woman.
Goodbye, American chick, goodbye, American broad.

American woman, get away from me,
American woman, mama let me be.
Don't come knockin' around my door,
Don't wanna see your shadow no more.
Colored lights can hypnotize,
Sparkle someone else's eyes.
Now woman, I said get away,
American woman, listen what I say.

American woman, said get away,
American woman, listen what I say.
Don't come hangin' around my door,
Don't wanna see your face no more.
I don't need your war machines,
I don't need your ghetto scenes.
Colored lights can hypnotize,
Sparkle someone else's eyes.
Now woman, get away from me,
American woman, mama let me be.

Annie's Song

Words and Music by John Denver

recorded by John Denver

You fill up my senses,
Like a night in a forest,
Like the mountains in springtime,
Like a walk in the rain.
Like a storm in the desert,
Like a sleepy blue ocean.
You fill up my senses,
Come fill me again.

Come let me love you,
Let me give my life to you,
Let me drown in your laughter,
Let me die in your arms.
Let me lay down beside you,
Let me always be with you,
Come let me love you,
Come love me again.

Repeat Verse 1

(Hey, Won't You Play) Another Somebody Done Somebody Wrong Song

Words and Music by Larry Butler and Chips Moman

recorded by B.J. Thomas

It's lonely out tonight
And the feelin' just got right
For a brand new love song,
Somebody done somebody wrong song.

Refrain:
Hey, won't you play
Another somebody done somebody wrong song,
And make me feel at home
While I miss my baby, while I miss my baby.

So play, play for me a sad melody,
So sad that it makes ev'rybody cry.
A real hurtin' song about a love that's gone wrong,
'Cause I don't wanna cry all alone.

Refrain

Anticipation

Words and Music by Carly Simon

recorded by Carly Simon

We can never know about the days to come,
But we think about them anyway.
And I wonder if I'm really with you now,
Or just chasing after some finer day.

Refrain:
Anticipation, anticipation is making me late,
Is keeping me waiting.

And I tell you how easy it feels to be with you.
And how right your arms feel around me.
But I, I rehearsed those words just late last night,
When I was thinking about how right tonight might be

Refrain

And tomorrow we might not be together.
I'm no prophet, I don't know nature's ways.
So I'll try and see into your eyes right now,
And stay right here, 'cause these are the good old days.
These are the good old days.

And stay right here, 'cause these are the good old days.
These are the good old days.
These are the good old days.
These are the good old days.
These are the good old days.

Baby Come Back

Words and Music by John C. Crowley and Peter Beckett

recorded by Player

Spendin' all my nights, all my money goin' out on the town.
Doin' anything just to get you off of my mind.
But when the morning comes, I'm right back where I started again.
And try'n to forget you is just a waste of time.

Refrain:
Baby, come back, any kind of fool could see
There was something in everything about you.
Baby, come back, you can blame it all on me.
I was wrong and I just can't live without you.

All day long wearin' a mask of false bravado,
Tryin' to keep up a smile that hides a tear.
Just as the sun goes down, I get that empty feeling again.
How I wish to God that you were here.

Refrain

Now that I've pulled it all together,
Give me the chance to make you see.
Have you used up all the love in your heart?
Nothin' left for me, ain't there nothin' left for me?

Refrain

I was wrong and I just can't live…

Refrain

At Seventeen

Words and Music by Janis Ian

recorded by Janis Ian

I learned the truth at seventeen;
That love was meant for beauty queens,
And high school girls with clear-skinned smiles,
Who married young and then retired.
The valentines I never knew,
The Friday night charades of youth,
Were spent on one more beautiful;
At seventeen, I learned the truth.

And those of us with ravaged faces,
Lacking in the social graces,
Desperately remained at home.
Inventing lovers on the phone,
Who called to say, "Come dance with me,"
And murmured vague obscenities.
It isn't all it seems
At seventeen.

A brown-eyed girl in hand-me-downs,
Whose name I never could pronounce,
Said, "Pity, please, the ones who serve.
They only get what they deserve.
The rich-relationed home town queen
Marries into what she needs,
A guarantee of company
And haven for the elderly."

Remember those who win the game,
Lose the love they sought to gain,
In debentures of quality,
And dubious integrity.
Their small town eyes will gape at you,
In dull surprise when payment due
Exceeds accounts received
At seventeen.

To those of us who know the pain
Of valentines that never came,
And those whose names were never called,
When choosing sides for basketball.
It was long ago and far away.
The world was younger than today,
And dreams were all they gave for free,
To ugly duckling girls like me.

We all play the game and when we dare
To cheat ourselves at solitaire,
Inventing lovers on the phone,
Repenting other lives unknown,
That call and say, "Come dance with me,"
And murmur vague obscenities,
At ugly girls like me;
At seventeen.

Babe

Words and Music by Dennis DeYoung

recorded by Styx

Babe, I'm leavin'. I must be on my way.
The time is drawing near.
My train is going, I see it in your eyes.
The love beneath your tears.

But I'll be lonely without you
And I'll need your love to see me through.
So please believe me, my heart is in your hand
And I'll be missing you.

'Cause you know it's you, babe,
Whenever I get weary and I've had enough.
Feel like giving up.
You know it's you, babe,
Giving me the courage and the strength I need
Please believe that it's true,
Babe, I love you.

Ahh, ahh, ahh, ahh,
Ahh, ahh, ahh, ahh, ahh, ahh.

You know it's you, babe,
Whenever I get weary and I've had enough.
Feel like giving up.
You know it's you, babe,
Giving me the courage and the strength I need
Please believe that it's true,
Babe, I love you.

Babe, I'm leavin'. I'll say it once again
And somehow try to smile.
I know the feeling we're trying to forget
If only for awhile.

'Cause I'll be lonely without you
And I'll need your love to see me through.
But please believe me, my heart is in your hands
'Cause I'll be missing you.
Babe I love you. Babe, I love you,
Ooh, ooh babe.

Baby, I Love Your Way

Words and Music by Peter Frampton

recorded by Peter Frampton

Shadows grow so long before my eyes,
And they're moving across the page.
Suddenly the day turns into night,
Far away from the city.
But don't hesitate 'cause your love won't wait.

Refrain:
Ooh, baby I love your way everyday.
Wanna tell you I love your way everyday.
Wanna be with you night and day.

Moon appears to shine and light the sky
With the help of some firefly.
Wonder how they have the power to shine.
I can see them under the pine.
But don't hesitate 'cause your love won't wait.

Refrain

But don't hesitate 'cause your love won't wait.

I can see the sunset in your eyes
Brown and gray and blues besides.
Clouds are stalking islands in the sun,
Wish I could buy one out of season.
But don't hesitate 'cause your love won't wait.

Refrain Twice

Baby, I'm-A Want You

Words and Music by David Gates

recorded by Bread

Baby, I'm a-want you.
Baby, I'm a-need you.
You the only one I care enough to hurt about.
Maybe I'm a-crazy, but I just can't live without
Your lovin' and affection, givin' me direction,
Like a guiding light to help me through my darkest hour.
Lately I'm a-prayin' that you'll always be a-stayin' beside me.

Used to be my life was just emotions passing by,
Feeling all the while and never really knowing why.

Lately I'm a-prayin' that you'll always be a-stayin' beside me.

Used to be my life was just emotions passing by.
Then you came along and made me laugh and made me cry.
You taught me why.

Baby, I'm a-want you.
Baby, I'm a-need you.
Oh, it took so long to find you, baby.
Baby, I'm a-want you.
Baby, I'm a-need you.

Bad, Bad Leroy Brown

Words and Music by Jim Croce

recorded by Jim Croce

Well the south side of Chicago
Is the baddest part of town,
And if you go down there
You better just beware
Of a man name of Leroy Brown.
Now Leroy more than trouble,
You see he stand 'bout six-foot four;
All the downtown ladies call him "Tree-top" lover
All the men just call him, "Sir."

Refrain:
And he's bad, bad Leroy Brown,
The baddest man in the whole damned town;
Badder than old King Kong
And meaner than a junk-yard dog.

Now Leroy he a gambler,
And he like his fancy clothes.
And he like to wave his diamond rings
In front of everybody's nose.
He got a custom Continental,
He got a Eldorado too;
He got a thirty-two gun
In his pocket for fun,
He got a razor in his shoe.

Refrain

Well, Friday 'bout a week ago,
Leroy shootin' dice.
And at the edge of bar sat a girl name of Doris
And oh, that girl looked nice.
Well, he cast his eyes upon her,
And the trouble soon began,
And Leroy Brown, he learned a lesson
'Bout messin' with the wife of a jealous man.

Refrain

Well, the two men took to fightin',
And when they pulled them from the floor,
Leroy looked like a jig-saw puzzle
With a couple of pieces gone.

Refrain

Yes, you were badder than old King Kong,
And meaner than a junk-yard dog.

Ben

Words by Don Black
Music by Walter Scharf

recorded by Michael Jackson

Ben, the two of us need look no more,
We both found what we were looking for.
With a friend to call my own,
I'll never be alone,
And you my friend will see,
You've got a friend in me.

Ben, you're always running here and there,
You feel you're not wanted anywhere.
If you ever look behind,
And don't like what you find,
There's something you should know,
You've got a place to go.

I used to say I and me,
Now it's us, now it's we.
I used to say I and me,
Now it's us, now its we.
Ben, most people would turn you away,
I don't listen to a word they say.
They don't see you as I do,
I wish they would try to.
I'm sure they'd think again if they had a friend like Ben,

Like Ben, like Ben, like Ben, like Ben.

Best Thing That Ever Happened to Me

Words and Music by Jim Weatherly

recorded by Gladys Knight & The Pips

I've had my share of life's ups and downs,
But fate's been kind, the downs have been few.
I guess you could say that I've been lucky,
And I guess you could say it's all because of you.

Refrain:
If anyone should ever write my life story,
For whatever reason there might be,
You'd be there between each line of pain and glory,
'Cause you're the best thing that ever happened to me.
You're the best thing that ever happened to me.

Lord, there have been times when the times were hard,
But always somehow I made it through.
But for every moment I've spent hurting,
There was a moment spent loving you.

Refrain

Bennie and the Jets

Words and Music by Elton John and Bernie Taupin

recorded by Elton John

Hey, kids, shake it loose together.
The spotlight's hitting something that's been known to change the
    weather.
We'll kill the fatted calf tonight, so stick around.
You're gonna hear electric music, solid walls of sound.

Say, Candy and Ronnie, have you seen them yet,
Ooh, but they're so spaced out.
B-B-B-B-B Bennie and the Jets.
Oh but they're weird and they're wonderful.
Oh, Bennie, she's really keen.
She's got electric boots, a mohair suit;
You know I read it in a magazine, oh.

B-B-B Bennie and the Jets.

Hey, kids, plug into the faithless.
Maybe their blinded, but Bennie makes them ageless.
We shall survive; let us take ourselves along,
Where we fight our parents out in the streets
To find who's right and who's wrong.

Say, Candy and Ronnie, have you seen them yet,
Ooh, but they're so spaced out.
B-B-B-B-B Bennie and the Jets.
Oh but they're weird and they're wonderful.
Oh, Bennie, she's really keen.
She's got electric boots, a mohair suit;
You know I read it in a magazine, oh.

B-B-B Bennie and the Jets.

Repeat and Fade:
Bennie, Bennie, Bennie,
Bennie and the Jets.

Best of My Love

Words and Music by John David Souther, Don Henley and Glenn Frey

recorded by The Eagles

Every night
I'm lying in bed,
Holdin' you close in my dreams;
Thinkin' about all the things that we said
And comin' apart at the seams.
We try to talk it over
But the words come out too rough;
I know you were tryin'
To give me the best of your love.

Beautiful faces,
Loud empty places
Look at the way that we live,
Wastin' our time
On cheap talk and wine
Left us so little to give.

The same old crowd
Was like a cold dark cloud
That we could never rise above,
But here in my heart
I give you the best of my love.

Oh, sweet darlin',
You get the best of my love,
(You get the best of my love.)
Oh, sweet darlin',
You get the best of my love.
(You get the best of my love.)

I'm goin' back in time
And it's a sweet dream.
It was a quiet night
And I would be alright
If I could go on sleeping.

But every morning
I wake up and worry
What's gonna happen today.
You see it your way,
And I see it mine,
But we both see it slippin' away.

You know, we always had each other, baby.
I guess that wasn't enough.
Oh, but here in my heart
I give you the best of my love.
Oh, sweet darlin',
You get the best of my love.
Oh, sweet darlin',
You get the best of my love.

Bless the Beasts and Children

Words and Music by Barry DeVorzon and Perry Botkin, Jr.

from *Bless the Beasts and Children*
recorded by Carpenters

Bless the beasts and the children,
For in this world they have no voice,
They have no choice.
Bless the beasts and the children,
For the world can never be,
The world they see.

Refrain:
Light their way
When the darkness surrounds them;
Give them love, let it shine all around them.
Bless the beasts and the children;
Give them shelter from a storm;
Keep them safe;
Keep them warm.

Refrain

Bless the beasts and the children;
Give them shelter from a storm;
Keep them safe;
Keep them warm.

Blue Eyes Crying in the Rain

Words and Music by Fred Rose

recorded by Willie Nelson

In the twilight glow I see her
Blue eyes crying in the rain.
As we kissed good-bye and parted
I knew we'd never meet again.

Love is like a dying ember.
Only memories remain.
Through the ages I'll remember
Blue eyes crying in the rain.

Now my hair has turned to silver.
All my life I've loved in vain.
I can see her star in heaven,
Blue eyes crying in the rain.

Someday when we meet up yonder,
We'll stroll hand in hand again
In a land that knows no parting,
Blue eyes crying in the rain.

Blue Bayou

Words and Music by Roy Orbison and Joe Melson

recorded by Linda Ronstadt

I feel so bad, I've got a worried mind;
I'm so lonesome all the time,
Since I left my baby behind on Blue Bayou.
Saving nickels, saving dimes;
Working 'til the sun don't shine;
Looking forward to happier times on Blue Bayou.

I'm going back someday,
Come what may, to Blue Bayou,
Where you sleep all day
And the catfish play on Blue Bayou.
All those fishing boats with their sails afloat;
If I could only see
That familiar sunrise through sleepy eyes,
How happy I'd be.

Go to see my baby again
And to be with some of my friends;
Maybe I'd be happy then on Blue Bayou.
Saving nickels, saving dimes;
Working 'til the sun don't shine;
Looking forward to happier times on Blue Bayou.

I'm going back someday,
Gonna stay on Blue Bayou,
Where the folks are fine
And the world is mine on Blue Bayou.
Ah, that girl of mine by my side,
The silver moon and the evening tide,
Oh, some sweet day,
Gonna take away this hurtin' inside.

I'll never be blue;
My dreams come true
On Blue Bayou.

Bohemian Rhapsody

Words and Music by Freddie Mercury

recorded by Queen

Is this the real life? Is this just fantasy?
Caught in a landslide, no escape from reality.
Open your eyes, look up to the skies and see,
I'm just a poor boy, I need no sympathy,
Because I'm easy come, easy go, little high, little low,
Any way the wind blows doesn't really matter to me, to me.

Mama, just killed a man
Put a gun against his head, pulled my trigger, now he's dead.
Mama, life had just begun,
But now I've gone and thrown it all away.

Mama, ooh,
Didn't mean to make you cry.
If I'm not back again this time tomorrow, carry on,
Carry on as if nothing really matters.

Too late, my time has come,
Sends shivers down my spine, body's aching all the time.
Goodbye, ev'rybody I've got to go,
Gotta leave you all behind and face the truth.

Mama, ooh,
I don't want to die,
I sometimes wish I'd never been born at all.

I see a little silhouetto of a man,
Scaramouche, Scaramouche, will you do the Fandango.

Chorus:
Thunderbolt and lightning,
very, very frightening me. (Galileo.)
Galileo. (Galileo)
Galileo, Galileo, Figaro, magnifico.

Solo: I'm just a poor boy and nobody loves me.
Chorus: He's just a poor boy from a poor family.
Spare him his life from this monstrosity.
Solo: Easy come, easy go, will you let me go, Bismillah!

Chorus:
No, we will not let you go. (Let him go!)
Bismillah! We will not let you go. (Let him go!)
Bismillah! We will not let you go. (Let me go.)
Will not let you (Let me go) Will not let you go.
(Let me go.)

No, no, no, no, no, no, no.
Solo: Oh, mama mia, mama mia.
Chorus: Mama mia, let me go.
Beelzebub has a devil put aside for me, for me, for me.

So you think you can stone me and spit in my eye.
So you think you can love me and leave me to die.
Oh, baby, can't do this to me, baby,
Just gotta get out, Just gotta get right outta here.

Nothing really matters, anyone can see,
Nothing really matters, nothing really matters to me.
Any way the wind blows.

Brand New Key

Words and Music by Melanie Safka

recorded by Melanie

I rode my bicycle past your window last night
I roller skated to your door at daylight.
It almost seems like you're avoiding me.
I'm okay alone, but, you got something I need.

Refrain:
Well I got a brand new pair of roller skates, you got a brand new key.
I think that we should get together and try them out, you see.
I been looking around awhile, you got something for me.
Oh, I got a brand new pair of roller skates, you got a brand new key.

I ride my bike, I roller skate, don't drive no car.
Don't go too fast, but I go pretty far.
For somebody who don't drive I been all around the world.
Some people think I done all right for a girl.

Refrain

I asked your mother if you were at home.
She said, "Yes" but you weren't alone.
Well, sometimes I think that you're avoiding me.
I'm okay alone but, you got something I need.

Refrain

Celebrate

Words and Music by Alan Gordon and Garry Bonner

recorded by Three Dog Night

Slippin' away, sittin' on a pillow,
Waitin' for night to fall.
A girl and a dream sittin' on a pillow,
This is the night to go to the celebrity ball.

Satin and lace, isn't it a pity,
Didn't find time to call.
Ready or not, gonna make it to the city,
This is the night to go to the celebrity ball.

Dress up tonight,
Why be lonely?
You'll stay late and you'll be alone,
So why be lonely?

Refrain (Twice):
Sittin' alone, sittin' on a pillow,
Waitin' to climb the walls.
Maybe tonight, depending how your dream goes,
She'll open your eyes when she goes to the celebrity ball.

Celebrate, celebrate, dance to the music!
Celebrate, celebrate, dance to the music!

Can't Smile Without You

Words and Music by Chris Arnold, David Martin and Geoff Morrow

recorded by Barry Manilow

You know I can't smile without you.
I can't smile without you.
I can't laugh and I can't sing.
I'm findin' it hard to do anything.
You see, I feel sad when you're sad.
I feel glad when you're glad.
If you only knew what I'm goin' through.
I just can't smile without you.

You came along just like a song,
And brightened my day.
Who'd've believed that you were part of a dream?
Now it all seems light years away.

And now you know, I can't smile without you.
I can't smile without you.
I can't laugh and I can't sing.
I'm findin' it hard to do anything.
You see, I feel sad when you're sad.
I feel glad when you're glad.
If you only knew what I'm going through.
I just can't smile.

Now, some people say happiness takes
So very long to find.
Well, I'm findin' it hard
Leavin' your love behind me.

And you see, I can't smile without you.
I can't smile without you.
I can't laugh and I can't sing.
I'm findin' it hard to do anything.
You see, I feel sad when you're sad.
I feel glad when you're glad.
If you only knew what I'm going through.
I just can't smile.

Repeat and Fade:
Can't smile without you.
Can't smile without you.
Can't laugh and I can't sing.
I'm findin' it hard to do anything.

Carry On Wayward Son

Words and Music by Kerry Livgren

recorded by Kansas

Carry on my wayward son;
There'll be peace when you are done.
Lay your weary head to rest;
Don't you cry no more.

Once I rose above the noise and confusion
Just to get a glimpse beyond this illusion.
I was soaring ever higher,
But I flew too high.

Though my eyes could see,
I still was a blind man.
Though my mind could think,
I still was a mad man.
I hear voices when I'm dreaming.
I can hear them say:

Refrain:
Carry on my wayward son;
There'll be peace when you are done.
Lay your weary head to rest;
Don't you cry no more.

Masquerading as a man with a reason,
My charade is the event of the season.
And if I claim to be a wise man,
It surely means that I don't know.

On a stormy sea of moving emotion,
Tossed about, I'm like a ship on the ocean.
I set a course for winds of fortune,
But I hear the voices say:

Refrain

Carry on; you will always remember.
Carry on; nothing equals the splendor.
Now your life's no longer empty;
Surely heaven waits for you.

Refrain

Chevy Van

Words and Music by Sammy Johns

recorded by Sammy Johns

I gave a girl a ride in my wagon;
She crawled in and took control.
She was tired; as her mind was a-dragging,
I said, "Get some sleep and dream of rock and roll."

Refrain:
'Cause like a picture she was laying there,
Moonlight dancing off her hair.
She woke up and took me by the hand.
She's gonna love me in my Chevy van
And that's alright with me.

Her young face was like that of an angel,
Her long legs were tanned and brown.
Better keep your eyes on the road, son.
Better slow this vehicle down.

Refrain

I put her out in a town that was so small
You could throw a rock from end to end.
A dirt road street, she walked off in bare feet.
It's a shame I won't be passing through again.

Refrain

(They Long to Be) Close to You

Lyric by Hal David
Music by Burt Bacharach

recorded by Carpenters

Why do birds suddenly appear
Every time you are near?
Just like me they long to be
Close to you.

Why do stars fall down from the sky
Every time you walk by?
Just like me they long to be
Close to you.

On the day that you were born
The angels got together
And decided to create a dream come true.
So they sprinkled moon-dust in your hair
And gold and starlight in your eyes of blue.

That is why all the boys [girls] in town
Follow you all around.
Just like me they long to be
Close to you.
Just like me they long to be
Close to you.

The Closer I Get to You

Words and Music by James Mtume and Reggie Lucas

recorded by Roberta Flack & Donny Hathaway

The closer I get to you,
The more you make me see;
By giving me all you've got,
Your love has captured me.
Over and over again,
I try to tell myself that we could never be more than friends;
And all the while inside I knew it was real,
The way you make me feel.

Repeat and Fade

Could It Be Magic

Inspired by "Prelude in C Minor" by F. Chopin
Words and Music by Barry Manilow and Adrienne Anderson

recorded by Barry Manilow

Spirit move me, every time I'm near you,
Whirling like a cyclone in my mind.
Sweet Melissa, angel of my lifetime,
Answer to all answers I can find;
Baby, I love you.

Refrain (Twice):
Come, come, come into my arms.
Let me know the wonder of all of you.
Baby, I want you.
Now, now, now and hold on fast.
Could this be the magic at last?
Lady take me high upon a hillside,
High up where the stallion meets the sun.
I could love you; building my world around you,
Never leave you till my life is done;
Baby, I love you.

Could it be magic?
Come, come, come into my arms.
Let me know the wonder of all of you.

Come and Get Your Love

Words and Music by Lolly Vegas

recorded by Redbone

Spoken:
Come and get your love. Come and get your love.
Come and get your love, now.
Come and get your love. Come and get your love.
Come and get your love.

Sung:
Yeah, (yeah,) what's the matter with your hair?
Oh, yeah. Yeah, (yeah,)
What's the matter with your mind
And your sign and a, oh, yeah.

Mmm, how I gonna get it, baby, gonna get my lovin'?
Talk to me how I gonna get it.
I'm ready for you, baby, ready for your lovin'.
Don't make me wait 'cause I really need to get it.

Yeah, (yeah,) whip it baby, 'cause you're fine
And you're mine and you look so divine.
Come and get your love.
Come and get your love.

Spoken: Come and get your love.
Sung: Come and get your love.
Oh, yeah. Come and get your love.

Yeah, (yeah,) what's the matter with ya?
Feel right, don't you feel right, baby?
Yeah, (yeah,) whoa, get it from the main vine, alright.

Mmm, how I gonna get it, baby, gonna get my lovin'?
Talk to me how I gonna get it.
I'm ready for you, baby, ready for your lovin'.
Don't make me wait 'cause I really need to get it.

Yeah, (yeah,) it's your business.
If you want some, take some, get it together, baby.
Come and get your love.
Come and get your love.

Spoken: Come and get your love.
Sung: Come and get your love.
Oh, yeah. Come and get your love.

Come and get your love. Come and get your love.
Come and get your love, now.
Come and get your love. Come and get your love.
Come and get your love, now.

Mmm, what'cha waitin' for 'cause I'm ready for your lovin'.
Come and take it. Come and get it if you want it.
What's the matter? What's the problem?
Get together and we're easy gonna solve it.

Repeat and Fade:
Come and get your love. Come and get your love.
Spoken: Come and get your love.
Sung: Come and get your love.
Whoa, yeah. Come and get your love.

Come Sail Away

Words and Music by Dennis DeYoung

recorded by Styx

I'm sailing away.
Set an open course for the virgin sea.
'Cause I've got to be free,
Free to face the life that's ahead of me.
On board I'm the captain, so climb aboard.
We'll search for tomorrow on every shore,
And I'll try, oh Lord, I'll try to carry on.

I look to the sea.
Reflections in the waves spark my memory.
Some happy, some sad,
I think of childhood friends and the dreams we had.
We lived happily forever, so the story goes,
But somehow we missed out on the pot of gold.
But we'll try best that we can to carry on.

A gathering of angels appeared above my head.
They sang to me this song of hope, and this is what they said.
They said, "Come sail away, come sail away,
Come sail away with me, lads.
Come sail away, come sail away,
Come sail away with me.
Come sail away, come sail away,
Come sail away with me.
Come sail away, come sail away,
Come sail away with me."

I thought that they were angels, but to my surprise,
We climbed aboard their starship; we headed for the skies,
Singin', "Come sail away, come sail away,
Come sail away with me."

Da Ya Think I'm Sexy

Words and Music by Rod Stewart and Carmine Appice

recorded by Rod Stewart

She sits alone, waiting for suggestions.
He's so nervous, avoiding all the questions.
His lips are dry, her heart is gently pounding.
Don't you just know exactly what they're thinking?

Refrain:
If you want my body and you think I'm sexy,
Come on, sugar, let me know.
If you really need me, just reach out and touch me.
Come on, honey, tell me so.

He's acting shy, looking for an answer.
"Come on, honey, let's spend the night together."
"Now, hold on a minute before we go much further.
Give me a dime so I can phone my mother."
They catch a cab to his high-rise apartment.
At last he can tell her exactly what his heart meant.

Refrain

His heart's beating like a drum,
'Cause at last he's got this girl home.
Relax, baby. Now we're all alone.

They wake at dawn, 'cause all the birds are singing.
Two total strangers, but that ain't what they're thinking.
Outside it's cold, misty, and it's raining.
They got each other. Neither one's complaining.
He says, "I'm sorry, but I'm out of milk and coffee."
"Never mind, sugar. We can watch the early movie."

Refrain

Daddy Don't You Walk So Fast

Words and Music by Peter Callender and Geoff Stephens

recorded by Wayne Newton

The love between the two of us was dyin'.
And it got so bad I knew I had to leave.
But halfway down the highway when I turned around I saw
My little daughter runnin' after me, cryin',

Refrain:
"Daddy don't you walk so fast.
Daddy don't you walk so fast.
Daddy slow down some, 'cause you're makin' me run.
Daddy don't you walk so fast."

It broke my heart to tell my little daughter
That her daddy had to run and catch a train.
She had no way of knowing I was leavin' home for good.
I turned around and there she was again, cryin',

Refrain

If only for the sake of my sweet daughter,
I just had to turn back home right there and then,
And try to start a new life with the mother of my child.
I couldn't bear to hear those words again, as she said,

Refrain

"Won't you slow down some
'Cause you're makin' me run.
Daddy don't you walk so fast."

Do That to Me One More Time

Words and Music by Toni Tennille

recorded by Captain & Tennille

Do that to me one more time,
Once is never enough with a man like you.
Do that to me one more time,
I can never get enough of a man like you.
Whoa, kiss me like you just did.
Oh, baby, do that to me once again.

Pass that by me one more time,
Once just isn't enough for my heart to hear.
Tell it to me one more time,
I can never hear enough while I got'cha near.
Whoa, say those words again like you just did.
Oh, baby, tell it to me once again.

Dancing Queen

Words and Music by Benny Andersson, Bjorn Ulvaeus and Stig Anderson

from *Mamma Mia!*
recorded by ABBA

Refrain:
You can dance, you can jive,
Having the time of your life.
Oh, see that girl. Watch that scene,
Diggin' the dancing queen.

Friday night and the lights are low.
Looking out for a place to go,
Oh, where they play the right music.
Getting in the swing, you come to look for a king.

Anybody could be that guy.
Night is young and the music's high.
With a bit of rock music,
Everything is fine.

You're in the mood for a dance,
And when you get the chance,
You are the dancing queen,
Young and sweet, only seventeen.
Dancing queen, feel the beat from the tambourine.

Refrain

You're a teaser. You turn 'em on,
Leave 'em burning and then you're gone,
Looking out for another.
Anyone will do.

You're in the mood for a dance,
And when you get the chance,
You are the dancing queen,
Young and sweet, only seventeen.
Dancing queen, feel the beat from the tambourine.

Refrain

Repeat and Fade:
Diggin' the dancing queen.

December 1963
(Oh, What a Night)

Words and Music by Robert Gaudio and Judy Parker

recorded by The Four Seasons

Oh, what a night, late December back in sixty-three.
What a very special time for me,
As I remember what a night.

Oh, what a night. You know I didn't even know her name,
But I was never gonna be the same.
What a lady, what a night.

Refrain:
I got a funny feelin' when she walked in the room
And my, as I recall, it ended much too soon.
Oh, what a night.

Hypnotizing, mesmerizing' me,
She was ev'rything I dreamed she'd be.
Sweet surrender, what a night.

Why'd it take so long to see the light?
Seemed so wrong, but now it seems so right.
What a lady, what a night.

Refrain

I felt a rush like a rolling ball of thunder
Spinnin' my head around and takin' my body under.
Oh, what a night.

Repeat Four Times and Fade:
Do, do, do do, do, do, do, do, do,
Oh, what a night.
Do, do, do do, do, do, do, do, do,
Oh, what a night.

Diary

Words and Music by David Gates

recorded by Bread

I found her diary underneath the tree
And started reading about me.
The words she'd written took me by surprise.
You'd never read them in her eyes.
They said that she had found the love she's waited for.
Wouldn't you know it. She wouldn't show it.

Then she confronted with the writing there,
Simply pretending not to care.
I passed it off as just in keeping with
Her total disconcerting air.
And though she tried to hide
The love that she denied.
Wouldn't you know it, She wouldn't show it.

And as I go through my life
I will give to her my wife,
All the sweet things I can find.

I found her diary underneath a tree
And started reading about me.
The words began to stick, then tears to fall.
Her meaning now was clear to see.
The love she's waited for was someone else, not me.
Wouldn't you know it,
She wouldn't show it.

And as I go through my life
I will wish for her, his wife,
All the sweet things she can find,
All the sweet things she can find.

Do You Know Where You're Going To?

Words by Gerry Goffin
Music by Mike Masser

Theme from *Mahogany*
recorded by Diana Ross

Refrain:
Do you know
Where you're going to?
Do you like the things that life is showing you?
Where are you going to?
Do you know?

Do you get
What you're hoping for?
When you look behind you there's no open door.
What are you hoping for,
Do you know?

Once we were standing still in time,
Chasing the fantasies that filled our minds.
And you knew
How I loved you but my spirit was free,
Laughing at the questions that you once asked of me.

Refrain

No looking back at all we planned,
We let so many dreams just slip through our hands.
Why must we wait so long before we see
How sad the answers to those questions can be?

Refrain

Do You Wanna Make Love

Words and Music by Peter McCann

recorded by Peter McCann

Sometimes the love rhymes that fill the afternoon
Lose all the meaning with the rising moon.
So hold me and tell me that the words you say are true,
Answer the question I must ask of you.

Refrain:
Do you wanna make love, or do you just wanna fool around?
I guarantee it will bring you down if you try to fool yourself.
Do you wanna make love, or do you just wanna fool around?
You can take it seriously, or take it somewhere else.

Take all the freedom that a lover will allow
If you feel the feeling that I'm feeling now.
Where love goes a fool knows that the hurt can go as deep,
Don't make a promise that you cannot keep.

Refrain

But, if you wanna get close to me,
You could do it so easily.
Is it love that I see when I look in your eyes
Or just another empty lie?

Repeat

Don't Cry Out Loud
(We Don't Cry Out Loud)

Words and Music by Peter Allen and Carole Bayer Sager

recorded by Melissa Manchester

Baby cried the day the circus came to town,
'Cause she didn't like parades just passing by her.
So she painted on a smile and took up with some clown,
And she danced without a net, up on the wire.
I know a lot about her 'cause you see,
Baby is an awful lot like me.

Refrain:
Don't cry out loud,
Just keep it inside,
Learn how to hide out feelings.
Fly high and proud.
And if you should fall,
Remember you almost had it all.

Baby cried the day they pulled the big top down,
They left behind her dreams among the litter.
And the different kind of love she thought she found,
Was nothing more than sawdust and some glitter.
But baby can't be broken 'cause you see,
She had the finest teacher, that was me.
I told her—

Refrain

Don't Give Up on Us

Words and Music by Tony Macaulay

recorded by David Soul

Don't give up on us, baby,
Don't make the wrong seem right,
The future isn't just one night,
It's written in the moonlight
And painted on the stars,
We can't change ours.

Don't give up on us, baby
We're still worth one more try,
And though we put the last one by,
Just for a rainy evening
When maybe stars are few.

Don't give up on us, baby
I know we can still come through.
I nearly lost my head last night,
You've got a right to stop believing.
There's still a little love left even so.

Don't give up on us, baby
Lord knows we've come this far,
Why can't we stay the way we are?
The angel and the dreamer
Who sometimes plays a fool.

Don't give up on us, I know
We can still come through.
It's written in the moonlight
And painted on the stars,
We can't change ours.

Don't give up on us, baby,
We're still worth one more try,
And though we put a last one by,
Just for a rainy evening
When stars are few.

Don't give up on us, I know
We can still come through.
Don't give up on us, baby,
Don't give up on us, baby.

Don't Go Breaking My Heart

Words and Music by Carte Blanche and Ann Orson

recorded by Elton John & Kiki Dee

Male: Don't go breaking my heart.
Female: I couldn't if I tried.
Male: Oh, honey, if I get restless
Female: Baby, you're not that kind.

Male: Don't go breaking my heart.
Female: You take the weight off me.
Male: Oh, honey, when you knock on my door
Female: Ooh, I gave you my key.

Both: Ooh, hoo, nobody knows it,
Male: But when I was down,
Female: I was your clown.
Both: Ooh, hoo, nobody knows it, nobody knows it
Male: But right from the start,
Female: I gave you my heart.
Oh, oh, I gave you my heart.

Male: So don't go breaking my heart.
Female: I won't go breaking your heart.
Both: Don't go breaking my heart.

Male: And nobody told us,
Female: 'Cause nobody showed us.
Male: And now it's up to us, babe.
Female: Whoa, I think we can make it.

Male: So don't misunderstand me.
Female: You put the light in my life.
Male: Oh, you put the spark to the flame.
Female: I got your heart in my sights.

Both: Ooh, hoo, nobody knows it,
Male: But when I was down,
Female: I was your clown.
Both: Ooh, hoo, nobody knows it, nobody knows it,
Male: But right from the start,
Female: I gave you my heart.
Oh, oh, I gave you my heart.

Male: Don't go breaking my heart.
Female: I won't go breaking your heart.
Both: Don't go breaking my heart.

Ooh, hoo, nobody knows it,
Male: But when I was down,
Female: I was your clown,
Male: And right from the start,
Female: I gave you my heart.
Oh, oh, I gave you my heart.

Male: Don't go breaking my heart.
Female: I won't go breaking your heart.
Both: Don't go breaking my heart.
Female: I won't go breaking your heart.

Male: Don't go breaking my heart.
Female: I won't go breaking your heart.
Male: Don't go breaking my heart.
Female: I won't go breaking your heart.

Don't Let the Sun Go Down on Me

Words and Music by Elton John and Bernie Taupin

recorded by Elton John

I can't light
No more of your darkness.
All my pictures
Seem to fade to black and white.
I'm growing tired
And time stands still before me.
Frozen here,
On the ladder of my life.

Too late
To save myself from falling.
I took a chance
And changed your way of life.
But you misread
My meaning when I met you.
Closed the door
And left me blinded by the light.

Don't let the sun go down on me.
Although I search myself,
It's always someone else I see.
I'd just allow a fragment of your life
To wander free.
But losing everything
Is like the sun going down on me.

I can't find
Oh, the right romantic line.
But see me once,
And see the way I feel.
Don't discard me
Just because you think I mean you harm.
But these cuts I have,
Oh, they need love
To help them heal.

Don't let the sun go down on me.
Although I search myself,
It's always someone else I see.
I'd just allow a fragment of your life
To wander free.
But losing everything
Is like the sun going down on me.

Don't Pull Your Love

Words and Music by Dennis Lambert and Brian Potter

recorded by Hamilton, Joe Frank & Reynolds

Refrain:
Don't pull your love out on me, baby.
If you do then I think that maybe
I'll just lay me down, cry for a hundred years.
Don't pull your love out on me, honey.
Take my heart, my soul, my money,
But don't leave me a-drownin' in my tears.

You say you're gonna leave,
Gonna take that big white bird,
Gonna fly right out of here without a single word.
But you know you'll break my heart
When I want to close the door.
'Cause I know I won't see you anymore.

Refrain

Haven't I been good to you?
What about that brand new ring?
Doesn't that mean love to you?
Doesn't that mean anything?
If I threw away my pride and I got down on my knees,
Would you make me beg you pretty please?

Refrain

There's so much I wanna do.
I've got love enough for two.
But I'll never use it, girl,
If I don't have you.

Refrain

Dream Weaver

Words and Music by Gary Wright

recorded by Gary Wright

I've just closed my eyes again,
Climbed aboard the dream weaver train.
Driver, take away my worries of today
And leave tomorrow behind.

Refrain:
Ooh, dream weaver,
I believe you can get me through the night.
Ooh, dream weaver,
I believe we can reach the morning light.

Fly me high through the starry skies,
Or maybe to an astral plane.
Cross the highways of fantasy,
Help me to forget today's pain.

Refrain

Though the dawn may be coming soon,
There still may be some time.
Fly me away to the bright side of the moon
And meet me on the other side.

Refrain

Dream weaver, dream weaver.

Dreams

Words and Music by Stevie Nicks

recorded by Fleetwood Mac

Now, here you go again.
You say you want your freedom.
Well who am I to keep you down?
It's only right that you should play the way you feel it.
But listen carefully to the sound of your loneliness,
Like a heart-beat, drives you mad,
In the stillness of remembering what you had
And what you lost and what you had and what you lost.

Refrain:
Oh, thunder only happens when it's raining.
Players only love you when their playing.
Say, women, they will come and they will go.
When the rain washes you clean, you'll know.
You'll know.

Now, here I go again.
I see the crystal vision.
I keep my visions to myself.
It's only me who wants to wrap around your dreams.
And have you any dreams you'd like to sell.
Dreams of loneliness, like a heart-beat, drives you mad,
In the stillness of remembering what you had
And what you lost and what you had and what you lost.

Refrain

You will know. Oh, you will know.

Dust in the Wind

Words and Music by Kerry Livgren

recorded by Kansas

I close my eyes
Only for a moment, and the moment's gone.
All my dreams
Pass before my eyes, a curiosity.
Dust in the wind.
All they are is dust in the wind.

Same old song.
Just a drop of water in an endless sea.
All we do
Crumbles to the ground though we refuse to see.
Dust in the wind.
All we are is dust in the wind.

Don't hang on.
Nothing lasts forever but the earth and sky.
It slips away.
All your money won't another minute buy.
Dust in the wind.
All we are is dust in the wind.
All we are is dust in the wind.
Dust in the wind.
Everything is dust in the wind.
Everything is dust in the wind.

Easy

Words and Music by Lionel Richie

recorded by The Commodores

Know it sounds funny, but I just can't stand the pain;
Girl, I'm leaving you tomorrow.
Seems to me, girl, you know I've done all I can.
You see, I begged, stole, and I borrowed, yeah.

Refrain:
Ooh, that's why I'm easy.
I'm easy like Sunday morning.
That's why I'm easy.
I'm easy like Sunday morning.

Why in the world would anybody put chains on me?
I've paid my dues to make it.
Everybody wants me to be what they want me to be.
I'm not happy when I try to fake it, no.

Refrain

I wanna be high, so high.
I wanna be free to know the things I do are right.
I wanna be free, just me, oh, babe.

Repeat and Fade:
That's why I'm easy.
I'm easy like Sunday morning.
That's why I'm easy.
I'm easy like Sunday morning.

Even Now

Lyric by Marty Panzer
Music by Barry Manilow

recorded by Barry Manilow

Even now when there's someone else who cares,
When there's someone home who's waiting just for me.
Even now I think about you as I'm climbing up the stairs,
And I wonder what to do so she won't see…

That even now I know it wasn't right,
And I've found a better life than what we had.
Even now I wake up crying in the middle of the night,
And I can't believe it still could hurt so bad.

Even now when I have come so far,
I wonder where you are,
I wonder why it's still so hard without you,
Even now when I come shining through,
I swear I think of you, and how much I wish you knew
Even now.

Even now when I never hear your name,
And the world has changed so much since you've been gone.
Even now I still remember and the feeling's still the same,
And the pain inside of me goes on and on.
Even now.

Repeat Verse 3

Feel Like Makin' Love

Words and Music by Eugene McDaniels

recorded by Roberta Flack

Strollin' in the park,
Watchin' winter turn to spring.
Walkin' in the dark,
Seein' lovers do their thing.

Refrain:
That's the time
I feel like makin' love to you.
That's the time
I feel like makin' dreams come true.
Oh, baby.
When you talk to me,
When you're moanin' sweet and low.
When you're touchin' me
And my feelings start to show.

Refrain

In a restaurant,
Holdin' hands by candlelight.
While I'm touchin' you,
Wanting you with all my might.

Refrain

Repeat Verse 1 and Refrain

The First Cut Is the Deepest

Words and Music by Cat Stevens

recorded by Rod Stewart

I would have given you all of my heart,
But there's someone who's torn it apart.
And she's [he's] taken just all that I had.
But if you want, I'll try to love again.

Refrain:
Baby, I'll try to love again, but I know:
The first cut is the deepest.
Baby, I know the first cut is the deepest.
When it comes to bein' lucky, she's cursed;
When it comes to lovin' me, she's [he's] worst.

I still want you by my side,
Just to help me dry the tears that I've cried.
And I'm sure gonna give you a try,
And if you want, I'll try to love again.

Refrain

I still want you by my side,
Just to help me dry the tears that I've cried.
And I'm sure gonna give you a try,
And if you want, I'll try to love again.

Refrain

The First Time Ever I Saw Your Face

Words and Music by Ewan MacColl

recorded by Roberta Flack

The first time ever I saw your face,
I thought the sun rose in your eyes,
And the moon and the stars were the gifts you gave
To the dark and the end of the skies.

The first time ever I kissed your mouth,
I felt the earth move in my hand,
Like the trembling heart of a captive bird
That was there at my command,

The first time ever I lay with you
And felt your heart so close to mine,
And I knew our joy would fill the earth
And last till the end of time, my love.
The first time ever I saw your face.

Fly Like an Eagle

Words and Music by Steve Miller

recorded by Steve Miller Band

Tick, tock, tick. Doot, doot, do, do…

Time keeps on slippin', slippin', slippin' into the future
Time keeps on slippin', slippin', slippin' into the future.

I wanna fly like an eagle to the sea.
Fly like an eagle, let my spirit carry me.
I want to fly like an eagle till I'm free.
Oh, Lord, through the revolution.

Feed the babies who don't have enough to eat.
Shoe the children with no shoes on their feet.
House the people livin' in the street.
Oh, there's a solution.

I want to fly like an eagle to the sea.
Fly like an eagle, let my spirit carry me.
I want to fly like an eagle till I'm free.
Right through the revolution.

Four Times:
Time keeps on slippin', slippin', slippin' into the future.

Do, dootn' do, do...

I want to fly like an eagle to the sea.
Fly like an eagle, let my spirit carry me.
I want to fly like an eagle till I'm free.
Right through the revolution.

Tick, tock, tick. Doot, doot, do, do...

Repeat and Fade:
Time keeps on slippin', slippin', slippin' into the future.

For All We Know

Words by Robb Wilson and Arthur James
Music by Fred Karlin

from the Motion Picture *Lovers and Other Strangers*
recorded by Carpenters

Love, look at the two of us, strangers in many ways.
We've got a lifetime to share,
So much to say, and as we go from day to day,
I'll feel you close to me, but time alone will tell.
Let's take a lifetime to say, "I knew you well,"
For only time will tell us so,
And love may grow for all we know.

Love, look at the two of us, strangers in many ways.
Let's take a lifetime to say, "I knew you well,"
For only time will tell us so,
And love may grow for all we know.

Goodbye to Love

Words and Music by Richard Carpenter and John Bettis

recorded by Carpenters

I'll say goodbye to love.
No one ever cared if I should live or die.
Time and time again the chance for love has passed me by,
And all I know of love is how to live without it.
I just can't seem to find it.
So I've made my mind up I must live my life alone.
And though it's not the easy way,
I guess I've always known I'd say

Goodbye to love.
There are no tomorrows for this heart of mine.
Surely time will lose these bitter memories and I'll find,
That there is someone to believe in and to live for.
Something I could live for.
All the years of useless search have finally reached an end,
And loneliness and empty days will be my only friend.
From this day love is forgotten and I'll go on as best I can.

What lies in the future is a mystery to us all,
No one can predict the wheel of fortune as it falls,
There may come a time when I will see that I've been wrong.
But for now this is my song.
And it's goodbye to love,
I'll say goodbye to love.

Garden Party

Words and Music by Rick Nelson

recorded by Ricky Nelson

I went to a garden party
To reminisce with my old friends,
A chance to share old memories
And play our songs again.
When I go to the garden party,
They all knew my name,
But no one recognized me,
I didn't look the same.

Refrain:
But it's alright now,
I learned my lesson well.
You see, you can't please ev'ry one,
So you got to please yourself.

People came for miles around,
Ev'ryone was there.
Yoko brought her walrus,
There was magic in the air.
And over in the corner,
Much to my surprise,
Mister Hughes hid in Dylan's shoes,
Wearing his disguise.

Refrain

I played them all the old songs,
I thought that's why they came;
No one heard the music,
We didn't look the same.
I said hello to "Mary Lou,"
She belongs to me.
When I sang a song 'bout a honky tonk,
It was time to leave.

Refrain

Someone opened up a closet door,
And out stepped Johnny B. Good,
Playing guitar like ringin' a bell
And lookin' like he should.
If you gotta play at garden parties,
I wish you a lot of luck,
But if memories were all I sang,
I'd rather drive a truck.

Refrain

Goodbye Yellow Brick Road

Words and Music by Elton John and Bernie Taupin

recorded by Elton John

When are you gonna come down?
When are you going to land?
I should have stayed on the farm.
I should have listened to my old man.
You know you can't hold me forever.
I didn't sign up with you
I'm not a present for your friends to open.
This boy's too young to be singing the blues. Ah, ah.

Refrain:
So goodbye yellow brick road,
Where the dogs of society howl.
You can't plant me in your penthouse.
I'm going back to my plough,
Back to the howling old owl in the woods,
Hunting the horny-backed toad.
Oh, I've fin'ly decided my future lies
Beyond the yellow brick road. Ah, ah.

What do you think you'll do then?
I bet they'd shoot down the plane.
It'll take you a couple of vodka and tonics
To set you on your feet again.
Maybe you'll get a replacement.
There's plenty like me to be found,
Mongrels who ain't got a penny
Sniffing for tidbits like you on the ground. Ah, ah.

Refrain

Goodnight Tonight

Words and Music by Paul McCartney

recorded by Wings

Don't get too tired for love,
Don't let it end.
Don't say goodnight to love,
It may never be the same again.

Refrain (Twice):
Don't say it! Don't say it!
Say anything but don't say goodnight tonight!
Don't say it! Don't say it!
Say anything but don't say goodnight tonight!
Don't say it! Don't say it!
You can say anything, but don't say goodnight tonight!

Don't get too tired for love,
Don't let it end.
Don't say goodnight to love,
It's a feeling that may never end.

Repeat and Fade:
Don't say it! Don't say it!
Say anything but don't say goodnight tonight!

Got to Be There

Words and Music by Elliott Willensky

recorded by Michael Jackson

Got to be there, got to be there in the morning,
When she says hello to the world.
Got to be there, got to be there,
Bring her good times and show her that she's my girl.

Refrain:
Oh, what a feeling there'll be
The moment I know she loves me.
'Cause when I look in her eyes,
I realize I need her sharing the world beside me.

So, I've got to be there, got to be there in the morning,
And welcome her into my world,
And show her that she's my girl.
When she says hello world, got to be there.

Got to be there, got to be there when she needs someone
To keep her through the night.
Got to be there, got to be there,
To take her hand and lead her into my life.

Refrain

That's why I've got to be there, got to be there
Where love begins and that's ev'rywhere she goes.
I've got to be there so she knows
That when she's with me she's home.

Repeat and Fade:
Got to be there, got to be there, got to be there.

Happy Days

Words by Norman Gimbel
Music by Charles Fox

Theme from the Paramount Television Series *Happy Days*
recorded by Pratt and McClain

Sunday, Monday, happy days!
Tuesday, Wednesday, happy days!
Thursday, Friday, happy days!
Saturday, what a day, rocking all week with you.

This day is ours.
Won't you be mine?
This day is ours.
Oh, please be mine.

Hello sunshine, goodbye rain.
She's wearing my school ring on a chain.
She's my steady, I'm her man.
I'm gonna love her all I can.

This day is ours.
Won't you be mine?
This day is ours.
Oh, please be mine.

These happy days are yours and mine.
These happy days are yours and mine, happy days!

Got to Get You into My Life

Words and Music by John Lennon and Paul McCartney

recorded by The Beatles; Earth, Wind & Fire

I was alone, I took a ride,
I didn't know what I would find there.
Another road where maybe I
Could see another kind of mind there.
Ooh, then suddenly I see you,
Ooh, did I tell you I need you
Every single day of my life?

You didn't run, you didn't lie,
You knew I just wanted to hold you.
And had you gone, you knew in time
We'd meet again for I had told you.
Ooh, you were meant to be near me,
Ooh, and I want you to hear me
Say we'll be together every day.

Got to get you into my life.

What can I do, what can I be?
When I'm with you I want to stay there.
If I'm true I'll never leave,
And if I do I know the way there.
Ooh, then I suddenly see you.
Ooh, did I tell you I need you
Every single day of my life?

Got to get you into my life.
Got to get you into my life.

I was alone, I took a ride,
I didn't know what I would find there.
Another road where maybe I
Could see another kind of mind there.
Ooh, then suddenly I see you,
Ooh, did I tell you I need you
Every single day of my life?
What are you doing to my life?

Haven't Got Time for the Pain

Words and Music by Carly Simon and Jacob Brackman

recorded by Carly Simon

All those crazy nights when I cried myself to sleep;
Now melodrama never makes me weep anymore.
'Cause I haven't got time for the pain, I haven't got room for the pain,
I haven't the need for the pain, not since I've known you.

You showed me how, how to leave myself behind,
How to turn down the noise in my mind.
Now I haven't got time for the pain, I haven't got room for the pain,
I haven't the need for the pain, not since I've known you.

I haven't got time for the pain, I haven't got room for the pain,
I haven't the need for the pain.
Suffering was the only thing made me feel I was alive,
Thought that's just how much it cost to survive in this world.

'Til you showed me how, how to fill my heart with love,
How to open up and drink in all that white light pouring down from
    heaven.
I haven't got time for the pain, I haven't got room for the pain,
I haven't the need for the pain, not since I've known you.

Repeat and Fade:
I haven't got time for the pain. I haven't got room for the pain.
I haven't the need for the pain.

Here Comes That Rainy Day Feeling Again

Words and Music by Tony Macaulay, Roger Cook and Roger Greenaway

recorded by The Fortunes

Here comes that rainy day feeling again,
And soon my tears, they will be falling like rain.
It always seems to be a Monday;
Left over memories of Sunday always spent with you
Before the clouds appeared, and took away my sunshine.

Here comes that rainy day feeling again,
And I'll be dreaming of you, baby, in vain.
Your face is always on my mind, girl;
I'm hoping soon, you're gonna find, girl, your way back to me,
'Cause if you say you'll stay, the rainy days will go away.

Misty morning eyes, I'm trying to disguise the way I feel.
But I just can't hide it; people seem to know;
The loneliness must show.
I'm thinking of my pride but breaking up inside, girl

Here comes that rainy day feeling again,
And soon my tears, they will be falling like rain.
It always seems to be a Monday;
Left over memories of Sunday always spent with you
Before the clouds appeared, and took away my sunshine.

Repeat and Fade:
Here comes that rainy day feeling again.

Here You Come Again

Words by Cynthia Weil
Music by Barry Mann

recorded by Dolly Parton

Here you come again,
Just when I've begun to get myself together.
You waltz right in the door,
Just like you've done before,
And wrap my heart 'round your little finger.

Here you come again,
Just when I'm about to make it work without you.
You look into my eyes,
And lie those pretty lies,
And pretty soon I'm wond'rin' how I came to doubt you.

Bridge:
All you gotta do is smile that smile
And there go all my defenses.
Just leave it up to you and in a little while
You're messin' up my mind and fillin' up my senses.

Refrain:
Here you come again,
Lookin' better than a body has a right to,
And shakin' me up so that all I really know
Is here you come again,
And here I go.

Repeat Bridge and Refrain

Here I go.

(Your Love Keeps Lifting Me) Higher and Higher

Words and Music by Gary Jackson, Carl Smith and Raynard Miner

recorded by Jackie Wilson, Rita Coolidge

Your love is liftin' me higher
Than I've ever been lifted before.

Refrain:
Your love is liftin' me higher
Than I've ever been lifted before.
So keep it up, quench my desire,
And I'll be at your side forevermore.

Now once I was downhearted;
Disappointment was my closest friend.
But you came; he soon departed,
And he never showed his face again.

I'm so glad I finally found you;
You're that "one in a million" man.
When you wrap your lovin' arms around me,
I can stand up and face the world again.

Refrain

Higher Ground

Words and Music by Stevie Wonder

recorded by Stevie Wonder

People keep on learnin'.
Soldiers keep on warrin',
World keep on turnin'
'Cause it won't be too long.
Powers keep on lyin',
While you people keep on dyin'.
World keep on turnin'
'Cause it won't be too long.

Refrain:
I'm so darn glad he let me try it again,
'Cause my last time on earth I lived a whole world of sin.
I'm so glad that I know more than I knew then,
Gonna keep on tryin' till I reach the highest ground.

Lovers keep on lovin',
Believers keep on believin'.
Sleepers just stop sleepin'
'Cause it won't be too long.

Refrain

Repeat and Fade:
Till I reach my highest ground.
No one's gonna bring me down.

Hopelessly Devoted to You

Words and Music by John Farrar

from *Grease*
recorded by Olivia Newton-John

Guess mine is not the first heart broken.
My eyes are not the first to cry.
I'm not the first to know
There's just no gettin' over you.

I know I'm just a fool who's willin'
To sit around and wait for you.
But, baby can't you see
There's nothing else for me to do?
I'm hopelessly devoted to you.

But now there's nowhere to hide
Since you pushed my love aside.
I'm out of my head, hopelessly devoted to you,
Hopelessly devoted to you.

My head is sayin', "Fool, forget him."
My heart is sayin', "Don't let go.
Hold on to the end."
And that's what I intend to do.
I'm hopelessly devoted to you.

But now there's nowhere to hide
Since you pushed my love aside.
I'm out of my head, hopelessly devoted to you,
Hopelessly devoted to you.
Hopelessly devoted to you.

How Can You Mend a Broken Heart

Words and Music by Barry Gibb and Robin Gibb

recorded by Bee Gees

I can think of younger days when living for my life
Was everything a man could want to do.
I could never see tomorrow,
I was never told about the sorrow.

Refrain:
And how can you mend a broken heart?
How can you stop the rain from falling down?
How can you stop the sun from shining?
What makes the world go 'round?
How can you mend this broken man?
How can a loser ever win?
Please help me mend my broken heart
And let me live again.

I can still feel the breeze that rustles through the trees
And misty memories of days gone by.
We could never see tomorrow;
No one said a word about the sorrow.

Refrain

How Deep Is Your Love

Words and Music by Barry Gibb, Robin Gibb and Maurice Gibb

from the Motion Picture *Saturday Night Fever*
recorded by Bee Gees

I know your eyes in the morning sun.
I feel you touch me in the pouring rain.
And the moment that you wander far from me,
I wanna feel you in my arms again.
And you come to me on a summer breeze;
Keep me warm in your love,
Then you softly leave.

Refrain:
And it's me you need to show
How deep is your love?
How deep is your love?
How deep is your love?
I really mean to learn.
'Cause we're living in a world of fools,
Breaking us down
When they all should let us be.
We belong to you and me.

I believe in you.
You know the door to my very soul.
You're the light in my deepest, darkest hour;
You're my savior when I fall.
And you may not think I care for you
When you know down inside
That I really do.

Refrain

Hurting Each Other

Words by Peter Udell
Music by Gary Geld

recorded by Carpenters

No one in the world
Ever had a love as sweet as my love.
For nowhere in the world
Could there be a boy as true as you, love.
All my love I give gladly to you;
All your love you give gladly to me.
Tell me why then, oh, why should it be that
We go on hurting each other?
We go on hurting each other, making each other cry,
Hurting each other without ever knowing why.

Closer than the leaves
On a weepin' willow, baby we are.
Closer, dear, are we
Than the simple letters "A" and "B" are.
All my life I could love only you;
All your life you could love only me.
Tell my why then, oh, why should it be that
We go on hurting each other?
We go on hurting each other, making each other cry,
Hurting each other without ever knowing why.

Can't we stop hurting each other?
Gotta stop hurting each other, making each other cry,
Breaking each other's heart, tearing each other apart.

I Am Woman

Words by Helen Reddy
Music by Ray Burton

recorded by Helen Reddy

I am woman, hear me roar,
In numbers too big to ignore,
And I know too much to go back to pretend.
'Cause I've heard it all before,
And I've been down there on the floor,
No one's ever gonna keep me down again.

Refrain:
Oh, yes I am wise, but it's wisdom born of pain.
Yes, I paid the price, but look how much I gained.
If I have to I can do anything.
I am strong, I am invincible,
I am woman.

You can bend but never break me,
'Cause it only serves to make me,
More determined to achieve my final goal.
And I come back even stronger,
Not a novice any longer,
'Cause you've deepened the conviction in my soul.

Refrain

I am woman! I am woman!

I Don't Know How to Love Him

Words by Tim Rice
Music by Andrew Lloyd Webber

from *Jesus Christ Superstar*
recorded by Helen Reddy

I don't know how to love him
What to do, how to move him.
I've been changed, yes, really changed.
In these past few days when I've seen myself
I seem like someone else.
I don't know how to take this
I don't see why he moves me.
He's a man, he's just a man,
And I've had so many men before
In very many ways he's just one more.

Should I bring him down, should I scream and shout?
Should I speak of love, let my feelings out?
I never thought I'd come to this.
What's it all about?

Don't you think it's rather funny
I should be in this position?
I'm the one who's always been so calm and cool
No lover's fool
Running every show.
He scares me so.

I never thought I'd come to this.
What's it all about?

Yet if he said he loved me,
I'd be lost I'd be frightened.
I couldn't cope, just couldn't cope.
I'd turn my head, I'd back away,
I wouldn't want to know.
He scares me so.
I want him so.
I love him so.

I Feel the Earth Move

Words and Music by Carole King

recorded by Carole King

Refrain:
I feel the earth move under my feet;
I feel the sky come tumbling down;
I feel my heart start to tremblin'
Whenever you're around.

Ooh, baby, when I see your face
Mellow as the month of May,
Oh, darlin', I can't stand it
When you look at me that way.

Refrain

Ooh, darlin' when I'm near you
And you tenderly call my name,
I know that my emotions
Are something I just can't tame.
I just got to have you, baby.
Aah! Aah! Yeah,

Repeat and Fade:
I feel the earth move under my feet;
I feel the sky come tumbling down.

I Like Dreamin'

Words and Music by Kenny Nolan

recorded by Kenny Nolan

Refrain:
I like dreamin', 'cause dreamin' can make you mine.
I like dreamin', closin' my eyes and feelin' fine.
When the lights go down, I'm holdin' you so tight,
Gotcha in my arms, and it's paradise 'til the mornin' light.

I see us on the shore beneath the bright sunshine.
We walked along Saint Thomas beach a million times.
Hand in hand, two barefoot lovers kissin' in the sand.
Side by side, the tide rolls in,
I'm touchin' you, you're touching me,
If only it could be.

Refrain

Through each dream, how our love has grown.
I see us with our children and our happy home.
Little smiles, so warm and tender, lookin' up at us.
Blessed by love, the world we share
Until I wake, I reach for you, and you're just not there.

Refrain

I Honestly Love You

Words and Music by Peter Allen and Jeff Barry

recorded by Olivia Newton-John

Maybe I hang around here a little more than I should.
We both know I got somewhere else to go.
But I got somethin' to tell you that I never thought I would,
But I believe you really ought to know.
I love you.
I honestly love you.

You don't have to answer, I see it in your eyes.
Maybe it was better left unsaid.
But this is pure and simple and you must realize,
That it's comin' from my heart and not my head.
I love you.
I honestly love you.

I'm not tryin' to make you feel uncomfortable
I'm not tryin' to make you anything at all.
But this feeling doesn't come along every day,
And you shouldn't blow the chance,
When you've got the chance to say:
I love you.

Spoken:
I love you.
Sung:
I honestly love you.

If we both were born in another place and time,
This moment might be ending with a kiss.
But there you are with yours and here I am with mine,
So I guess we'll just be leaving it at this:
I love you.
I honestly love you.
I honestly love you.

I Will Survive

Words and Music by Dino Fekaris and Frederick J. Perren

recorded by Gloria Gaynor

At first I was afraid, I was petrified;
Kept thinkin' I could never live without you by my side.
But then, I spent so many nights thinkin' how you did me wrong
And I grew strong, and I learned how to get along.
And so you're back from outer space.
I just walk in to find you here with that sad look upon your face.
I should have changed that stupid lock, I should have made you leave
    your key,
If I'd've known for just one second you'd be back to bother me.

Refrain:
Go on, now go, walk out the door;
Just turn around now, 'cause you're not welcome anymore.
Weren't you the one who tried to hurt me with goodbye?
Did you think I'd crumble, did you think I'd lay down and die.
Oh, no, not I, I will survive.
Oh, as long as I know how to love, I know I'll stay alive.
I've go all my life to live, I've got all my love to give
And I'll survive, I will survive!

It took all the strength I had not to fall apart;
Kept tryin' hard to mend the pieces of my broken heart.
And I spent, oh, so many nights just feelin' sorry for myself,
I used to cry, but now I hold my head up high.
And you see me, somebody new,
I'm not that chained up little person still in love with you.
And so you felt like droppin' in and just expect me to be free.
Well now, I'm savin' all my lovin' for someone who's lovin' me.

Refrain

I Write the Songs

Words and Music by Bruce Johnston

recorded by Barry Manilow

I've been alive forever,
And I wrote the very first song.
I put the words and the melodies together,
I am music, and I write the songs.

Refrain:
I write the songs that make the whole world sing;
I write the songs of love and special things.
I write the songs that make the young girls cry;
I write the songs, I write the songs.

My home lies deep within you
And I've got my own place in your soul.
Now, when I look out through your eyes
I'm young again, even though I'm very old.

Refrain

Oh, my music makes you dance
And gives you a second chance,
And I wrote some rock 'n' roll
So you can move.

Music fills your heart,
Well, that's a real fine place to start.
It's from me, it's for you,
It's from you, it's for me
It's a world-wide symphony.

Refrain

I Wish

Words and Music by Stevie Wonder

recorded by Stevie Wonder

Looking back on when I was a little nappy headed boy.
Then my only worry was for Christmas what would be my toy.
Even though we sometimes would not get a thing,
We were happy with the joy the day would bring.

Sneakin' out the back door to hang out with those hoodlum friends of
   mine.
Ooh. Greeted at the back door with "Boy, I thought I told you not to go
   outside."
Tryin' your best to bring the water to your eyes,
Thinkin' it might stop her from whoopin' your behind.

I wish those days could come back once more.
Why did those days ever have to go?
I wish those days could come back once more.
Why did those days ever have to go, 'cause I loved them so.

Do do, do do, do, do, do, do, do , do, do, do,
Do do, do do, do, do, do, do do, do.

Brother says he's tellin' 'bout you playin' doctor with that girl.
Just don't tell, I'll give you anything you want in this whole wide world.
Mama gives you money for Sunday school.
You trade yours for candy after church is through.

Smokin' cigarettes and writin' something nasty on the wall.
Spoken: You nasty boy.
Sung: Teacher sends you to the principal's office down the hall.
You grow up and learn that kinda thing ain't right,
But while you were doin' it, it sure felt out-a sight.

I wish those days could come back once more.
Why did those days ever have to go?
I wish those days could come back once more.
Why did those days ever have to go.

I Won't Last a Day Without You

Words and Music by Paul Williams and Roger Nichols

recorded by Carpenters

Day after day,
I must face a world of strangers where I don't belong,
I'm not that strong.
It's nice to know,
That there's someone I can turn to who will always care,
You're always there,

Refrain:
When there's no getting over that rainbow,
When my smallest of dreams won't come true,
I can take all the madness the world has to give,
But I won't last a day without you.

So many times,
When the city seems to be without a friendly face,
A lonely place.
It's nice to know,
That you'll be there if I need you and you'll always smile,
It's all worthwhile,

Refrain

Touch me and I end up singing,
Troubles seem to up and disappear,
You touch me with the love you're bringing,
I can't really lose when you're near.

When you're near my love,
If all my friends have forgotten half their promises
They're not unkind, just hard to find.
One look at you,
And I know that I could learn to live without the rest,
I found the best.

Refrain Twice

I'll Be There

Words and Music by Berry Gordy, Hal Davis, Willie Hutch and Bob West

recorded by The Jackson 5

You and I must make a pact.
We must bring salvation back.
Where there is love,
I'll be there.
(I'll be there.)
I'll reach out my hand to you,
I'll have faith in all you do.

Refrain:
Just call my name
And I'll be there.
(I'll be there.)
I'll be there to comfort you,
Build my world of dreams around you.
I'm so glad I found you.
I'll be there with a love so strong.
I'll be your strength,
You know I'll keep holding on.

Let me fill your heart with joy and laughter.
Togetherness, well it's all I'm after.
Just call my name
And I'll be there.
(I'll be there.)
I'll be there to protect you
With an unselfish love that respects you.

Refrain

If you should ever find someone new,
I know she'd better be good to you,
'Cause if she doesn't,
Then I'll be there (I'll be there.)
Don't you know, baby.
I'll be there, I'll be there.
Just call my name and I'll be there.
I'll be there, I'll be there.
Just call my name and I'll be there.

I'll Have to Say I Love You in a Song

Words and Music by Jim Croce

recorded by Jim Croce

Well, I know it's kind of late.
I hope I didn't wake you.
But what I got to say can't wait.
I know you'd understand.

Refrain:
'Cause ev'ry time I tried to tell you
The words just came out wrong.
So I'll have to say I love you in a song.

Yeah, I know it's kind of strange,
But ev'ry time I'm near you,
I just run out of things to say.
I know you'd understand.

Refrain

'Cause ev'ry time the time was right
All the words just came out wrong.
So I'll have to say I love you in a song.

Yeah, I know it's kind of late.
I hope I didn't wake you.
But there's something that I just got to say.
I know you'd understand.

Refrain

I'll Never Love This Way Again

Words and Music by Richard Kerr and Will Jennings

recorded by Dionne Warwick

You looked inside my fantasies and made each one come true,
Something no one else had ever found a way to do.
I've kept the memories one by one, since you took me in.

Refrain:
I know I'll never love this way again.
I know I'll never love this way again,
So I keep holdin' on before the good is gone.
I know I'll never love this way again,
Hold on, hold on, hold on.
A fool will lose tomorrow reaching back for yesterday.
I won't turn my head in sorrow if you should go away.
I'll stand here and remember just how good it's been.
And…

Refrain

I know I'll never love this way again,
So I keep holdin' on before the good is gone.
I know I'll never love this way again,
Hold on, hold on, hold on.

If

Words and Music by David Gates

recorded by Bread

If a picture paints a thousand words,
Then why can't I paint you?
The words will never show
The you I've come to know.
If a face could launch a thousand ships,
Then where am I to go?
There's no one home but you,
You're all that's left me to.
And when my love for life is running dry,
You come and pour yourself on me.

If a man could be two places at one time,
I'd be with you;
Tomorrow and today,
Beside you all the way.
If the world should stop revolving,
Spinning slowly down to die,
I'd spend the end with you.
And when the world was through,
Then one by one, the stars would all go out.
Then you and I would simply fly away.

If You Leave Me Now

Words and Music by Peter Cetera

recorded by Chicago

If you leave me now,
You'll take away the biggest part of me.
Ooh, no, baby please don't go.
And if you leave me now,
You'll take away the very heart of me.
Ooh girl, I just want you to stay.

A love like ours is love that's hard to find.
How could we let it slip away?
We've come too far to leave it all behind.
How could we end it all this way?

When tomorrow comes,
Then we'll both regret the things we said today.

If you leave me now,
You'll take away the biggest part of me.
Ooh, no, baby please don't go.

Repeat Song

Repeat and Fade:
Ooh, girl, I just want to have you by my side.
Ooh, no, baby please don't go.

If Loving You Is Wrong I Don't Want to Be Right

Words and Music by Homer Banks, Carl Hampton and Raymond Jackson

recorded by Luther Ingram

If loving you is wrong, I don't want to be right.
If being right means being without you,
I'd rather live a wrong-doing life.
Your momma and daddy say it's a shame,
It's a down-right disgrace,
But, long as I got you by my side
I don't care what your people say.
Your friends tell you it's no future in loving a married man.
If I can't see you when I want, I'll see you when I can.

If loving you is wrong, I don't wanna be right.

Am I wrong to fall so deeply in love with you,
Knowing I got a wife and two little children
Depending on me too?
And am I wrong
To hunger for the gentleness of your touch,
Knowing I got someone else at home
Who needs me just as much?
And are you wrong to give your love to a married man?
And am I wrong to hold on to the best thing I ever had?

If loving you is wrong, I don't wanna be right.

Are you wrong to give your love to a married man?
And am I wrong for tryin' to hold on to the best thing I ever had?
If loving you is wrong, I don't wanna be right.
If loving you is wrong, I don't wanna be right.

Repeat and Fade:
I don't wanna be right, if it means being without you.
I don't wanna be right if it means sleeping at night.

If You're Ready (Come Go with Me)

Words and Music by Homer Banks, Carl Hampton and Raymond Jackson

recorded by The Staple Singers

If you're ready, come go with me.
If you're ready, come go with me.
If you're ready, come go with me.
Come go with me. Come go with me.
No hatred. Come go with me.
We'll be tolerated. Come go with me.
Peace and love. Come go with me;
Go between the races. Come go with me.
Love is the only transportation,
To where there's communication.

If you're ready, come go with me.
If you're ready, come go with me.
If you're ready, come go with me.
If you're ready, come go with me.
No hate. Come go with me,
Will ever enter there. Come go with me.
No one. Come go with me,
Will ever be sad. Come go with me.
No economical exploitation.
No political domination.

If you're ready, come go with me.
If you're ready, come go with me.
If you're ready, come go with me.
If you're ready, come go with me.
You citizens. Come go with me,
You'd better get ready. Come go with me.
Haters. Come go with me,
You'd better get ready. Come go with me.
Back stabbers. Come go with me,
You'd better get ready. Come go with me.
Come on get ready.

Repeat and Fade:
If you're ready, come go with me.
If you're ready, come go with me.

Imagine

Words and Music by John Lennon

recorded by John Lennon and the Plastic Ono Band

Imagine there's no heaven.
It's easy if you try.
No hell below us,
Above us only sky.
Imagine all the people
Living for today.

Imagine there's no countries.
It isn't hard to do.
Nothing to kill or die for
And no religion, too.
Imagine all the people
Living life in peace.

You may say I'm a dreamer.
But I'm not the only one.
I hope someday you'll join us
And the world will be as one.

Imagine no possessions.
I wonder if you can.
No need for greed or hunger,
A brotherhood of man.
Imagine all the people
Sharing all the world.

You may say I'm a dreamer.
But I'm not the only one.
I hope someday you'll join us
And the world will live as one.

It's Impossible (Somos novios)

English Lyric by Sid Wayne
Spanish Words and Music by Armando Manzanero

recorded by Perry Como

It's impossible,
Tell the sun to leave the sky.
It's just impossible.
It's impossible.
Ask a baby not to cry,
It's just impossible.
Can I hold you closer to me
And not feel you going through me?
Split the second that I never think of you?
Oh, how impossible.

Can the ocean keep from rushing to the shore?
It's just impossible.
If I had you
Could I ever want for more?
It's just impossible.
And tomorrow, should you
Ask me for the world
Somehow I'd get it.
I would sell my very soul and not regret it.
For to live without your love
Is just impossible,
Impossible,
Impossible.

It's Sad to Belong

Words and Music by Randy Goodrum

recorded by England Dan & John Ford Coley

Met you on a springtime day;
You were mindin' your life and I was mindin' mine too.
And lady when you looked my way,
I had a strange sensation, and darlin' that's when I knew,

Refrain:
Oh, it's sad to belong to someone else
When the right one comes along.
Yes, it's sad to belong to someone else
When the right one comes along.

Oh, I wake up in the night
And I reach beside me hopin' you will be there.
But instead I find someone who believed in me
When I said I'd always care.

Refrain

So, I'll live my life in a dream world
For the rest of my days.
Just you and me walking hand in hand
In a wishful memory.
Oh, I guess that's all that it will ever be.

I wish I had a time machine;
I could make myself go back until the day I was born.
And I would live my life again,
And rearrange it so that I'd be yours from now on.

Refrain

It's Too Late

Words and Music by Carole King and Toni Stern

recorded by Carole King

Stayed in bed all mornin' just to pass the time.
There's somethin' wrong here, there can be no denyin'.
One of us is changin' or maybe we've just stopped tryin'.

Refrain:
And it's too late, baby now, it's too late,
Though we really did try to make it.
Somethin' inside has died and I can't hide
And I just can't fake it.

It used to be so easy living here with you.
You were light and breezy and I knew just what to do.
Now you look so unhappy and I feel like a fool.

Refrain

There'll be good times again for me and you,
But we just can't stay together, don't you feel it too?
Still I'm glad for what we had and how I once loved you.

Refrain

It's too late, baby, it's too late,
Now, darlin', it's too late.

Joy to the World

Words and Music by Hoyt Axton

recorded by Three Dog Night

Jeremiah was a bullfrog,
Was a good friend of mine.
Never understood a single word he said,
But I helped him drink his wine.
Yes, he always had some mighty fine wine.
Singing:

Refrain:
Joy to the world.
All the boys and girls now.
Joy to the fishes in the deep blue sea,
Joy to you and me.

If I were the king of the world,
Tell you what I'd do.
Throw away the cars and the bars and the wars,
And make sweet love to you.
Yes, I'd make sweet love to you.
Singing:

Refrain

You know I love the ladies,
Love to have my fun.
I'm a high night flyer and a rainbow rider,
A straight shootin' son-of-a-gun.
Yes, a straight-shootin' son-of-a-gun.

Refrain Three Times and Fade

Laughter in the Rain

Words and Music by Neil Sedaka and Phil Cody

recorded by Neil Sedaka

Strolling along country roads with my baby,
It starts to rain, it begins to pour.
Without an umbrella we're soaked to the skin,
I feel a shiver run up my spine.
I feel the warmth of her hand in mine.

Refrain:
Oo, I hear laughter in the rain,
Walking hand in hand with the one I love.
Oo, how I love the rainy days
And the happy way I feel inside.

After a while we run under a tree,
I turn to her and she kisses me.
There with the beat of the rain on the leaves,
Softly she breathes and I close my eyes,
Sharing our love under stormy skies.

Refrain

Killing Me Softly with His Song

Words by Norman Gimbel
Music by Charles Fox

recorded by Roberta Flack

Refrain:
Strummin' my pain with his fingers,
Singin' my life with his words.
Killing me softly with his song,
Killing me softly with his song,
Tellin' my whole life with his words,
Killing me softly with his song.

I heard he sang a good song,
And I heard he had a style,
And so I went to see him
And listen for a while.
And there he was, this stranger,
There before my eyes.

Refrain

I felt all flushed with fever,
Embarrassed by the crowd.
I felt he found my letters
And read each one out loud.
I prayed that he would finish,
But he just kept right on.

Refrain

He sang as if he knew me
In all my dark despair.
And then he looked right through me
As if I wasn't there.
And he just kept on singing,
Singing clear and strong.

Refrain

Let It Be

Words and Music by John Lennon and Paul McCartney

recorded by The Beatles

When I find myself in times of trouble
Mother Mary comes to me
Speaking words of wisdom
Let it be.

And in my hour of darkness
She is standing right in front of me
Speaking words of wisdom
Let it be.

Let it be, let it be, let it be, let it be
Whisper words of wisdom
Let it be.

And when the broken-hearted people
Living in the world agree
There will be an answer
Let it be.

For though they may be parted there is
Still a chance that they will see
There will be an answer
Let it be.

Let it be, let it be, let it be, let it be
There will be an answer
Let it be.

And when the night is cloudy
There is still a light that shines on me
Shine until tomorrow
Let it be.

I wake up to the sound of music
Mother Mary comes to me
Speaking words of wisdom
Let it be.

Let it be, let it be, let it be, let it be
There will be an answer
Let it be.

Let it be, let it be, let it be, let it be
Whisper words of wisdom
Let it be...

Listen to What the Man Said

Words and Music by Paul and Linda McCartney

recorded by Wings

Any time, any day, you can hear the man say
That love is blind, well, I don't know
But I say love is kind.

Soldier boy kisses girl, leaves behind a tragic world,
But he won't mind, he's in love
And he says love is fine.

Oh, yes indeed we know
That people will find a way to go
No matter what the man said.

And love is fine for all we know,
For all we know our love will grow,
That's what the man said.
So won't you listen to what the man said.

Any time, any day, you can hear the man say
That love is blind, well, I don't know
But I say love is kind.

And love is fine for all we know,
For all we know our love will grow,
That's what the man said.
So won't you listen to what the man said.

The wonder of it all, baby,
The wonder of it all, baby,
The wonder of it all, baby,
Yeah, yeah, yeah.

The Long and Winding Road

Words and Music by John Lennon and Paul McCartney

recorded by The Beatles

The long and winding road that leads to your door,
Will never disappear, I've seen that road before.
It always leads me here, leads me to your door.

The wild and windy night that the rain washed away,
Has left a pool of tears crying for the day.
Why leave me standing here, let me know the way.

Many times I've been alone and many times I've cried,
Anyway, you'll never know the many ways I've tried.
But still they lead me back to the long and winding road.

You left me standing here a long, long time ago.
Don't leave me waiting here, lead me to you door.
Da da, da da …

Looks Like We Made It

Words and Music by Richard Kerr and Will Jennings

recorded by Barry Manilow

There you are,
Lookin' just the same as you did the last time I touched you.
And here I am,
Close to gettin' tangled up inside the thought of you.
Do you love him as much as I love her?
And will that love be strong when old feelings start to stir?
Looks like we made it.

Refrain:
Left each other on the way to another love.
Looks like we made it,
Or I thought so till today, until you were there, everywhere,
And all I could taste was love the way we made it.

Love's so strange,
Playing hide and seek with hearts and always hurting.
And we're the fools,
Standing close enough to touch those burning memories.
And if I hold you for the sake of all those times
Love made us lose our minds,
Could I ever let you go?
Oh no, we've made it.

Refrain

Oh, we made it. Looks like we made it. Looks like we made it.

My Eyes Adored You

Words and Music by Bob Crewe and Kenny Nolan

recorded by Frankie Valli

Refrain:
My eyes adored you.
Though I never laid a hand on you,
My eyes adored you.
Like a million miles away from me
You couldn't see how I adored you.
So close, so close and yet so far.

Carried your books from school,
Playin' make believe you're married to me.
You were fifth grade, I was sixth,
When we came to be.
Walkin' home every day
Over Barnegat Bridge and bay,
Till we grew into the me and you
Who went our separate ways.

Refrain

Headed for city lights,
Climbed the ladder up to fortune and fame.
Worked my fingers to the bone,
Made myself a name.
Funny, I seem to find
That no matter how the years unwind,
Still I reminisce 'bout the girl I miss
And the love I left behind.

Refrain

Love Will Keep Us Together

Words and Music by Neil Sedaka and Howard Greenfield

recorded by Captain & Tennille

Love will keep us together;
Think of me, babe, whenever
Some sweet-talkin' guy comes along,
Singin' his song.
Don't mess around;
You gotta be strong.

Refrain:
Just stop,
'Cause I really love ya;
Stop, I'll be thinkin' of ya.
Look in my heart and let love
Keep us together.

You, you belong to me now;
Ain't gonna set you free now.
When those guys start hangin' around,
Talkin' me down,
Hear with your heart
And you won't hear a sound.

Refrain

…Whatever.
Young and beautiful,
But someday your looks will be gone.
When others turn you off,
Who'll be turning you on?
I will, I will, I will.
I will be there to share forever;
Love will keep us together.
Said it before and I'll say it again,
While others pretend,
I need you now and I'll need you then.

Refrain

…Whatever.

Make It with You

Words and Music by David Gates

recorded by Bread

Hey, have you ever tried
Really reaching out for the other side?
I'm may be climbing on rainbows,
But baby, here goes.

Dreams, they're for those who sleep.
Life, it's for us to keep.
And if you're wondering
What this all is leading to,
I'd like to make it with you.
I really think that we could make it, girl.

No, you don't know me well,
And every little thing, only time will tell.
But you believe the things that I do
And we'll see it through.

Life can be short or long.
Love can be right or wrong.
And if I chose the one
I'd like to help me through,
I'd like to make it with you.
I really think that we can make it, girl.

Baby, you know that
Dreams, they're for those who sleep.
Life, it's for us to keep.
And if I chose the one
I'd like to help me through,
I'd like to make it with you.
I really think that we could make it, girl.

My Heart Belongs to Me

Words and Music by Alan Gordon

recorded by Barbra Streisand

I got the feelin' the feeling's gone,
My heart has gone to sleep.
One of these mornings I'll be gone.
My heart belongs to me.

Can we believe in fairy tales?
Can love survive when all else fails?
Can't hide the feelin' the feeling's gone.
My heart belongs to me.

But now my love, hey didn't I love you,
But we knew what had to be.
Somehow my love, I'll always love you,
But my heart belongs to me.

Put out the light and close your eyes,
Come lie beside me, don't ask why.
Can't hide the feelin' the feeling's gone.
My heart belongs to me.

(But now my love, hey didn't I love you?
Didn't I love you?
Didn't I love you?
Didn't I love you, baby?)

Don't cry, my love, I'll always love you,
But my heart belongs to me.
I got the feelin' the feeling's gone.
My heart belongs to me.

Neither One of Us (Wants to Be the First to Say Goodbye)

Words and Music by Jim Weatherly

recorded by Gladys Knight & The Pips

It's sad to think we're not gonna make it,
And it's gotten to the point where we just can't fake it,
But for some ungodly reason, we just won't let it die.
I guess neither one of us wants to be the first to say goodbye.

I keep wondering what I'll do without you.
And I guess you must be wondering that same thing too.
So we go on together living a lie,
Because neither one of us wants to be the first to say goodbye.

Every time I find the nerve to say I'm leavin',
Old memories get in the way.
Lord knows it's only me that I'm deceiving;
When it comes to say goodbye, that's a word I just can't say.

There can be no way this can have a happy ending.
So we just go on hurting and pretending,
And convincing ourselves to give it just on more try.
Because neither one of us wants to be the one to say goodbye;
Because neither one of us wants to be the first to say goodbye.

My Love

Words and Music by Paul and Linda McCartney

recorded by Paul McCartney & Wings

And when I go away
I know my heart can stay with my love.
It's understood
It's in the hands of my love,
And my love does it good,
Wo wo wo wo...
My love does it good.

And when the cupboard's bare,
I'll still find something there with my love.
It's understood
It's everywhere with my love,
And my love does it good,
Wo wo wo wo...
My love does it good.

Wo wo I love,
Oh wo, my love,
Only my love holds the other key to me,
Oh wo, my love,
Oh my love
Only my love does it good to me.
Wo wo wo wo...
My love does it good.

Don't ever ask me why
I never say goodbye to my love.
It's understood
It's everywhere with my love,
And my love does it good,
Wo wo wo wo...
My love does it good.

Wo wo, I love,
Oh wo, my love,
Only my love does it good to me.
Wo wo wo wo...

My Way

English Words by Paul Anka
Original French Words by Gilles Thibault
Music by Jacques Revaux and Claude Francois

a standard recorded by various artists

And now the end is near,
And so I face the final curtain.
My friend, I'll say it clear,
I'll state my case, of which I'm certain.
I've lived a life that's full,
I traveled each and ev'ry highway,
And more, much more than this,
I did it my way.

Regrets, I've had a few,
But then again, too few to mention.
I did what I had to do,
And saw it through without exception.
I planned each charted course,
Each careful step along the byway,
And more, much more than this,
I did it my way.

Yes, there were times, I'm sure you knew,
When I bit off more than I could chew.
But through it all, when there was doubt,
I ate it up and spit it out.
I faced it all, and I stood tall,
And did it my way.

I've loved, I've laughed and cried,
I've had my fill, my share of losing.
And now, as tears subside,
I find it all so amusing.
To think I did all that,
And may I say, not in a shy way,
"Oh no, oh, no, not me,
I did it my way."

For what is a man, what has he got?
If not himself, then he has naught.
To say the things he truly feels
And not the words of one who kneels,
The record shows I took the blows,
And did it my way.

Only Yesterday

Words and Music by Richard Carpenter and John Bettis

recorded by Carpenters

After long enough of being alone,
Everyone must face their share of loneliness.
In my own time, nobody knew
The pain I was goin' through,
And waitin' was all my heart could do.

Hope was all I had until you came.
Maybe you can't see how much you mean to me.
You were the dawn breaking the night,
The promise of morning light,
Filling the world surrounding me.

Refrain:
And when I hold you, baby, baby,
Feels like maybe things will be alright.
Baby, baby, your love's made me
Free as a song, singin' forever.
Only yesterday when I was sad and I was lonely,
You showed me the way to leave the past
And all its tears behind me.
Tomorrow may be even brighter than today,
Since I threw my sadness away,
Only yesterday.

I have found my home here in your arms;
Nowhere else on earth I'd really rather be.
Life waits for us; share it with me.
The best is about to be,
And so much is left for us to see.

Refrain

Only yesterday when I was sad and I was lonely,
You showed me the way to leave the past
And all its tears behind me.
Tomorrow may be even brighter than today,
Since I threw my sadness away,
Only yesterday.

Precious and Few

Words and Music by Walter D. Nims

recorded by Climax

Precious and few are the moments we two can share;
Quiet and blue like the sky I'm hung over you.
And if I can't find my way back home
It just wouldn't be fair
'Cause precious and few
Are the moments we two can share.

Baby, it's you on my mind, your love is so rare
Being with you is a feeling I just can't compare.
And if I can't hold you in my arms
It just wouldn't be fair,
'Cause precious and few
Are the moments we two can share.

Raindrops Keep Fallin' on My Head

Lyric by Hal David
Music by Burt Bacharach

from *Butch Cassidy and the Sundance Kid*
recorded by B.J. Thomas

Raindrops keep fallin' on my head,
And just like the guy whose feet are too big for his bed,
Nothin' seems to fit.
Those raindrops are fallin' on my head.
They keep fallin'.

So I just did me some talkin' to the sun.
And I said I didn't like the way he got things done.
Sleepin' on the job.
Those, raindrops are fallin' on my head.
They keep fallin'.

But there's one thing
I know
The blues they send to meet me
Won't defeat me.
It won't be long
Till happiness steps up to greet me.

Raindrops keep fallin' on my head,
But that doesn't mean my eyes will soon be turnin' red.
Cryin's not for me
'Cause I'm never gonna stop the rain by complainin'.
Because I'm free
Nothin's worryin' me.

Put Your Hand in the Hand

Words and Music by Gene MacLellan

recorded by Ocean

Refrain:
Put your hand in the hand
Of the man who stilled the water,
Put your hand in the hand
Of the man who calmed the sea;
Take a look at yourself,
And-a you can look at others differently,
By puttin' your hand in the hand
Of the man from a-Galilee.

Every time I look
Into the Holy Book, I wanna tremble
When I read about the part
Where a carpenter cleared the temple.
For the buyers and the sellers were no different fellas
Than what I profess to be,
And it causes me shame to know
I'm not the man that I should be!

Refrain

Mama taught me how to pray
Before I reached the age of seven.
And when I'm down on my knees
That's-a when I'm close to heaven.
Daddy lived his life with two kids and a wife
And he did what he could do,
And he showed me enough
Of what it takes to get you through.

Refrain

Rainy Days and Mondays

Lyrics by Paul Williams
Music by Roger Nichols

recorded by Carpenters

Talkin' to myself and feelin' old,
Sometimes I'd like to quit.
Nothing ever seems to fit.
Hangin' around, nothing to do but frown;
Rainy days and Mondays always get me down.

What I've got they used to call the blues,
Nothing is really wrong,
Feelin' like I don't belong.
Walkin' around, some kind of lonely clown;
Rainy days and Mondays always get me down.

Refrain:
Funny but it seems I always wind up here with you,
Nice to know somebody loves me.
Funny but it seems that it's the only thing to do,
Run and find the one who loves me.

What I feel has come and gone before,
No need to talk it out,
We know what it's all about.
Hangin' around, nothing to do but frown;
Rainy days and Mondays always get me down.

Refrain

What I feel has come and gone before,
No need to talk it out,
We know what it's all about.
Hangin' around, nothing to do but frown;
Rainy days and Mondays always get me down.

Hangin' around, nothing to do but frown;
Rainy days and Mondays always get me down.
Rainy days and Mondays always get me down.

Respect Yourself

Words and Music by Mack Rice and Luther Ingram

recorded by The Staple Singers

If you disrespect everybody that you run into,
How in the world do you think
Everybody s'posed to respect you?
If you don't give a heck
About the man with the Bible in his hand,
Just get out of the way and let the gentleman do his thing.
You the kind of gentleman want everything your way.
Take the sheet off your face, boy, it's a brand new day.
Respect yourself.

Refrain:
Respect yourself.
'Cause if you don't respect yourself
Ain't nobody gonna give a good,
Good hoot-e-nanny, boy!
Respect yourself, respect yourself.

If you're walking around thinking that the world
Owes you something 'cause you're here,
You're going out the world backward like you did
When you first came 'ere.
Keep talking about the president won't stop air pollution.
Put you hand over your mouth when you cough;
That'll help the solution.
You cuss around women folk, don't even know their name,
Then you're dumb enough to think it makes you a big ole man.

Refrain

She's a Lady

Words and Music by Paul Anka

recorded by Tom Jones

Well, she's all you'd ever want,
She's the kind men like to flaunt and take to dinner.
Well, she always know her place,
She's got style, she's got grace, she's a winner.

Refrain:
She's a lady,
Whoa, oh, oh, she's a lady,
Talkin' about that little lady,
And the lady is mine.

Well, she's never in the way,
Always something nice to say, what a blessing.
I can leave her on her own,
Knowing she's okay alone and there's no messing.

Refrain

Well, she never asks very much and I don't refuse her,
Always treat her with respect, I never would abuse her.
What she's got is hard to find and I don't want to lose her.
Help me build a mountain from a little pile of clay-ay-ay-ay!

She knows what I'm about,
She can take what I dish out and that's not easy.
Well, she know me thru and thru,
She knows what to do and how to please me.

Refrain

Reunited

Words and Music by Dino Fekaris and Freddie Perren

recorded by Peaches & Herb

I was a fool to ever leave your side.
Me minus you is such a lonely ride.
The break-up we had has made me lonesome and sad;
I realize I love you 'cause I want you bad, hey, hey!
I spent the evenings with the radio;
Regret the moment that I let you go.
Our quarrel was such a way of learning so much,
I know now that I love you 'cause I miss your kiss, hey, hey!

Refrain:
Reunited and it feels so good.
Reunited 'cause we understood,
There's one perfect fit and, sugar, this one is it.
We both are so excited, 'cause we're reunited, hey, hey!

I sat here staring at the same old wall.
Came back to life just when I got your call.
I wished I could climb right through the telephone line
And give you what you want so you would still be mine, hey, hey!
I can't go cheatin', honey, I can't play.
I found it very hard to stay away.
As we reminisce on precious moments like this,
I'm glad we're back together, 'cause I miss your kiss, hey, hey!

Refrain

Lover, lover, this is solid love,
And you're exactly what I'm dreaming of.
All through the day and all through the night,
I'll give you all the love I have with all my might, hey, hey!

Refrain

Ooh, listen baby, I won't ever make you cry,
I won't let one day go by
Without holding you, without kissing you,
Without loving you.
Ooh, you're my everything,
Only you know how to free all the love there is in me.
I wanna let you know, I won't let you go.
Ooh, feels so good!

Refrain

She Believes in Me

Words and Music by Steve Gibb

recorded by Kenny Rogers

While she lays sleeping,
I stay out late at night and play my songs.
And sometimes all the nights can be so long,
And it's good when I fin'lly make it home all alone.
While she lays dreaming,
I try to get undressed without the light.
Then quietly she says, "How was your night?"
And I come to her and say it was all right.
And I hold her tight.

And she believes in me.
I'll never know just what she sees in me.
I told her someday if she was my girl
I could change the world with my little songs.
I was wrong.

But she has faith in me.
And so I go on trying faithfully,
And who knows, maybe on some special night
If my song is right, I will find a way,
Find a way.

While she lays waiting
I stumble to the kitchen for bite.
Then I see my old guitar in the night,
Just waiting for me like a secret friend, and there's no end.
While she lays crying, I fumble with a melody or two.
Then I'm torn between the things that I should do.
Then she says to wake her up when I am through.
God, her love is true.

And she believes in me.
I'll never know just what she sees in me.
I told her someday if she was my girl
I could change the world with my little songs.
I was wrong.

But she has faith in me.
And so I go on trying faithfully,
And who knows, maybe on some special night
If my song is right, I will find a way,
While she waits, while she waits, for me.

Ships

Words and Music by Ian Hunter

recorded by Barry Manilow

We walked to the sea, just my father 'n' me,
And the dogs played around on the sand.
Winter cold cut the air, hangin' still everywhere.
Dressed in gray, did he say, "Hold my hand?"
I said, "Love's easier when it's far away."
We sat 'n' watched a distant light.

Refrain:
We're two ships that pass in the night,
We both smile and we say it's alright.
We're still here, it's just that we're out of sight,
Like those ships that pass in the night.

There's a boat on the line where the sea meets the sky;
There's another that rides far behind.
And it seems you and I are like strangers
A wide ways apart as we drift on through time.
He said, "It's harder now, we're far away.
We only read you when you write."

Refrain

Sing

Words and Music by Joe Raposo

from "Sesame Street"
recorded by Carpenters

Sing, sing a song.
Sing out loud, sing out strong.
Sing of good things, not bad.
Sing of happy, not sad.

Sing, sing a song,
Make it simple, to last your whole life long.
Don't worry that it's not good enough
For anyone else to hear;
Just sing, sing a song.

La la la la la...

Sing, sing a song.
Let the world sing along.
Sing of love there could be.
Sing for you and for me.

Sing, sing a song.
Make it simple, to last your whole life long.
Don't worry that it's not good enough
For anyone else to hear;
Just sing, sing a song.
Just sing, sing a song.
Just sing, sing a song.

La la la la la...

So Far Away

Words and Music by Carole King

recorded by Carole King

So far away!
Doesn't anybody stay in one place anymore?
It would be so fine to see your face at my door.
Doesn't help to know that you're just time away.
Long ago, I reached for you and there you stood.
Holding you again could only do me good.
How I wish I could, but you're so far away!

One more song about movin' along the highway.
Can't say much of anything that's new.
If I could only work this life out my way,
I'd rather spend it bein' close to you.
But you're so...

Repeat Verse 1

Yeah, you're so far away!
Travelin' around sure gets me down and lonely.
Nothin' else to do but close my mind.
I sure hope the road don't come to own me.
There's so many dreams I've yet to find.
But you're so far away!

Repeat Verses 1 and 2 and Fade

Somewhere in the Night

Words and Music by Will Jennings and Richard Kerr

recorded by Barry Manilow

Time, you found time enough to love,
And I found love enough to hold you.
So tonight I'll stir the fire you feel inside
Until the flames of love enfold you.
Layin' beside you, lost in the feeling,
So glad you opened my door.
Come with me, somewhere in the night we will know
Everything lovers can know.

Refrain:
You're my song, music too magic to end,
I'll play you over and over again.
Lovin' so warm, movin' so right,
Closin' our eyes, and feelin' alive,
We'll just go on burnin' bright,
Somewhere in the night.

You'll sleep when the mornin' comes.
And I'll lie and watch you sleepin'.
And you'll smile when you dream about the night,
Like it's a secret you've been keepin'.
Layin' beside you, lost in the feeling,
So glad you opened my door.

Refrain

We'll just go on burnin' bright,
Somewhere in the night.

Someone Saved My Life Tonight

Words and Music by Elton John and Bernie Taupin

recorded by Elton John

When I think of those east end lights,
Muggy nights,
The curtains drawn
In the little downstairs
Prima donna, lord, you really should have been there.
Sitting like a princess perched in her electric chair.
And it's one more beer
And I don't hear you anymore.
We've all gone crazy lately,
My friends out there rollin' the basement floor.

Refrain:
And someone saved my life tonight,
Sugar bear.
You almost had your hooks in me
Didn't you dear?
You nearly had me roped and tied,
Altar bound, hypnotized,
Sweet freedom whispered in my ear.
You're a butterfly,
And butterflies are free to fly,
Fly away high away bye bye.

I never realized the passing hours
Of evening showers,
A slip noose hanging in my darkest dreams.
I'm strangled by your haunted social scene
Just a pawn out-played by a dominating queen.
It's four-o'clock in the morning
Damn it!
Listen to me good.
I'm sleeping with myself tonight,
Saved in time, thank God my music's still alive.

Refrain

And I would have walked head on
Into the deep end of a river,
Clinging to your stocks and bonds,
Paying your H. P. demands forever.
They're coming in the morning with a truck
To take me home.
Someone saved my life tonight,
Someone saved my life tonight,
Someone saved my life tonight,
Someone saved my life tonight,
Someone saved my life tonight,
So save your strength
And run the field you play alone.

Refrain

Someone saved my life tonight,
Someone saved my life tonight.

Sometimes When We Touch

Words by Dan Hill
Music by Barry Mann

recorded by Dan Hill

You ask me if I love you,
And I choke on my reply.
I'd rather hurt you honestly
Than mislead you with a lie.
And who am I to judge you
On what you say or do?
I'm only just beginning
To see the real you.

Refrain:
And sometimes when we touch,
The honesty's too much,
And I have to close my eyes and hide.
I wanna hold you till I die,
Till we both break down and cry,
I wanna hold you
Till the fear in me subsides.

Romance and all its strategy
Leaves me battling with my pride
But through the insecurity
Some tenderness survives.
I'm just another writer
Still trapped within my truths;
A hesitant prize-fighter
Still trapped within my youth.

At times I'd like to break you
And drive you to your knees.
At times I'd like to break through
And hold you endlessly.

At times I understand you,
And I know how hard you've tried,
I've watched while love commands you,
And I've watched love pass you by.
At times I think we're drifters,
Still searching for a friend,
A brother or a sister.
But then the passion flares again.

Refrain

Sorry Seems to Be the Hardest Word

Words and Music by Elton John and Bernie Taupin

recorded by Elton John

What have I got to do to make you love me?
What have I got to do to make you care?
What do I do when lightning strikes me
And I wake to find that you're not there?
What do I do to make you want me?
What have I gotta do to be heard?
What do I say when it's all over?
Sorry seems to be the hardest word.

Refrain:
It's sad, (It's so sad.)
It's so sad.
It's a sad, sad situation,
And it's getting more and more absurd.
It's sad, (It's so sad.)
It's so sad.
Why can't we talk it over?
Always seems to me
That sorry seems to be the hardest word.

What do I do to make you love me?
What have I gotta do to be heard?
What do I do when lightning strikes me?
What have I got to do,
What have I got to do?
Sorry seems to be the hardest word.

Speak Softly, Love
(Love Theme)

Words by Larry Kusik
Music by Nino Rota

from the Paramount Picture *The Godfather*
recorded by Andy Williams

Speak softly, love, and hold me warm against your heart.
I feel your words, the tender, trembling moments start.
We're in a world our very own,
Sharing a love that only few have ever known.
Wine colored days warmed by the sun,
Deep velvet nights when we are one.

Speak softly, love, so no one hears us but the sky.
The vows of love we make will live until we die.
My life is yours, and all because
You came into my world with love so softly, love.

Superstition

Words and Music by Stevie Wonder

recorded by Stevie Wonder

Very superstitious, writing's on the wall.
Very superstitious, ladder's 'bout to fall.
Thirteen month old baby broke the looking glass.
Seven years of bad luck. The good things in your past.
When you believe in things that you don't understand then you suffer.
Superstition ain't the way.

Very superstitious, wash your face and hands.
Rid me of the problems. Do all that you can.
Keep me in a daydream. Keep me goin' strong.
You don't wanna save me. Sad is my song.
When you believe in things that you don't understand then you suffer.
Superstition ain't the way.

Very superstitious, nothing more to say.
Very superstitious, the devil's on his way.
Thirteen month old baby broke the looking glass.
Seven years of bad luck. The good things in your past.
When you believe in things that you don't understand then you suffer.
Superstition ain't the way.

Sweet Seasons

Words and Music by Carole King and Toni Stern

recorded by Carole King

Sometimes you win, sometimes you lose,
And sometimes the blues get a hold of you
Ah just when you thought you had made it.
All around the block people will talk,
But I want to give it all that I've got.
I just don't want, I don't want to waste it.

Refrain:
Talkin' 'bout sweet seasons on my mind.
Sure does appeal to me!
You know we can get there easily,
Just like a sailboat sailin' on the sea.

Sometimes you win, and sometimes you lose,
And most times you choose between the two
Ah wonderin', wonderin' if you have made it.

But I'll have some kids and make my plans,
And I'll watch the seasons running away,
And I'll build me a life in the open, a life in the country.

Refrain

Talkin' 'bout sweet seasons,
Talkin' 'bout sweet, sweet, sweet seasons.

Take Me Home, Country Roads

Words and Music by John Denver, Bill Danoff and Taffy Nivert

recorded by John Denver

Almost heaven, West Virginia,
Blue Ridge Mountains, Shenandoah River.
Life is old there, older than the trees,
Younger than the mountains growin' like a breeze.

Refrain:
Country roads, take me home
To the place I belong:
West Virginia, mountain momma,
Take me home, country roads.

All memories gather 'round her,
Miner's lady, stranger to blue water.
Dark and dusty, painted on the sky,
Misty taste of moonshine, teardrop in my eye.

Refrain

I hear her voice, in the mornin' hour she calls me,
The radio reminds me of my home far away,
And drivin' down the road I get a feelin'
That I should have been home yesterday,
Yesterday.

Refrain

Country roads, take me home.

Three Times a Lady

Words and Music by Lionel Richie

recorded by The Commodores

Thanks for the times that you've given me,
The memories are all in my mind.
And now that we've come to the end of our rainbow,
There's something I must say out loud:

Refrain:
You're once, twice, three times a lady,
And I love you,
Yes, your once, twice, three times a lady,
And I love you,
I love you.

When we are together, the moments I cherish,
With every beat of my heart,
To touch you, to hold you, to feel you, to need you,
There's nothing to keep us apart.

Refrain

Teach Your Children

Words and Music by Graham Nash

recorded by Crosby, Stills, Nash & Young

You who are on the road
Must have a code
That you can live by,
And so become yourself,
Because the past
Is just a goodbye.

Teach your children well;
Their father's hell
Did slowly go by.
And feed them on your dreams,
The one they pick,
The one you'll know by.

Refrain:
Don't you ever ask them why;
If they told you, you would cry,
So just look at them and sigh
And know they love you.

And you, of tender years,
Can't know the fears
That your elders grew by.
And so, please help them
With your youth,
They seek the truth
Before they die.

Sung behind previous verse:
(Can you hear and do you care?
Do you see,
You must be free,
To teach your children?
You'll believe they'll make a world
That we can live in.)

Teach your parents well;
Their children's hell
Will slowly go by.
And feed them on your dreams,
The one they pick,
The one you'll know by.

Refrain

The Tears of a Clown

Words and Music by Stevie Wonder, William "Smokey" Robinson and Henry Cosby

recorded by Smokey Robinson & The Miracles

Now if there's a smile upon my face
It's only there trying to fool the public;
But when it comes down to fool you,
Now honey that's quite a different subject.
Don't let my glad expression
Give you the wrong impression;
Really I'm sad,
Oh, sadder than sad,
You're gone and I'm hurt so bad,
Like a clown, I pretend to be glad.

Refrain:
Now there's some sad things known to man
But ain't too much sadder than
The tears of a clown,
When there's no one around.

Oh yeah, baby,
Now if I appear to be carefree,
It's only to camouflage my sadness;
In order to shield my pride
I try to cover this hurt with a show of gladness.
But don't let my show convince you
That I've been happy since you decided to go,
I need you so, I'm hurt and I want you to know,
But for others I put on a show.

Just like Pagliacci did,
I try to keep my sadness hid,
Smiling in the public eye
But in my lonely room I cry
The tears of clown.

Oh, yeah baby!
Now, if there's a smile on my face
Don't let my glad expression
Give you the wrong impression.
Don't let this smile I wear
Make you think that I don't care.

Tie a Yellow Ribbon Round the Ole Oak Tree

Words and Music by L. Russell Brown and Irwin Levine

recorded by Dawn featuring Tony Orlando

I'm comin' home, I've done my time,
Now I've got to know what is and isn't mine.
If you received my letter tellin' you I'd soon be free,
Then you'll know just what to do if you still want me,
If you still want me.

Refrain:
Tie a yellow ribbon round the ole oak tree,
It's been three long years, do ya still want me?
If I don't see a ribbon round the ole oak tree
I'll stay n the bus, forget about us, put the blame on me,
If I don't see a yellow ribbon round the ole oak tree.

Bus driver please look for me,
'Cause I couldn't bear to see what I might see.
I'm really still in prison and my love she holds the key,
A simple yellow ribbon's what I need to set me free,
I wrote and told her please.

Refrain

Now the whole damn bus is cheering and I can't believe I see
A hundred yellow ribbons round the ole oak tree.

Time in a Bottle

Words and Music by Jim Croce

recorded by Jim Croce

If I could save time in a bottle,
The first thing that I'd like to do,
Is to save every day 'til eternity passes away,
Just to spend them with you.

If I could make days last forever,
If words could make wishes come true,
I'd save every day like a treasure and then
I would spend them with you.

Refrain:
But there never seems to be enough time
To do the things you want to do
Once you find them.
I've looked round enough to know
That you're the one I want to go through time with.

If I had a box just for wishes,
And dreams that had never come true,
The box would be empty,
Except for the memory
Of how they were answered by you.

Refrain

Top of the World

Words and Music by John Bettis and Richard Carpenter

recorded by Carpenters

Such a feelin's comin' over me,
There is wonder in most everything I see,
Not a cloud in the sky got the sun in my eyes,
And I won't be surprised if it's a dream.
Everything I want the world to be,
Is now coming true especially for me,
And the reason is clear,
It's because you are here,
You're the nearest thing to heaven that I've seen.

Refrain:
I'm on the top of the world
Lookin' down on creation
And the only explanation I can find,
Is the love that I've found,
Ever since you've been around,
Your love's put me at the top of the world.

Something in the wind has learned my name,
And it's tellin' me that things are not the same,
In the leaves on the trees and touch of the breeze,
There's a pleasin' sense of happiness for me.
There is only one wish on my mind,
When this day is through I hope that I will find,
That tomorrow will be just the same for you and me,
All I need will be mine if you are here.

Refrain

Torn Between Two Lovers

Words and Music by Phillip Jarrell and Peter Yarrow

recorded by Mary MacGregor

There are times when a woman has to say what's on her mind,
Even though she knows how much it's gonna hurt.
Before I say another word let me tell you I love you.
Let me hold you close and say these words as gently as I can.

There's been another man that I've needed and I've loved,
But that doesn't mean I love you less.
And he knows he can't possess me, and he knows he never will.
There's just this empty place inside of me that only he can fill.

Refrain:
Torn between two lovers, feeling like a fool,
Loving both of you is breaking all the rules.
Torn between two lovers, feeling like a fool,
Loving you both is breaking all the rules.

You mustn't think you failed me just because there's someone else,
You were the first real love I ever had.
And all the things I ever said, I swear they still are true
For no one else can have the part of me I gave to you.

Refrain

I couldn't really blame you if you turned and walked away,
But with everything inside of me, I'm asking you to stay.

Refrain

Touch a Hand, Make a Friend

Words and Music by Carl Hampton, Homer Banks and Raymond Jackson

recorded by The Staple Singers

Can't you feel it in your bones, y'all?
A change is coming on.
From every walk of life,
People are seeing the light.
Can't you feel it in your hearts now?
A new thing is takin' shape;
Reach out, touch a hand, y'all.

Make a friend if you can.
Hey, what about you my friend?
Ain't time you come on in?
Live the united way.
Why don't you join us today?

It's being reflected,
In the attitudes of others just like you.
Reach out touch a hand, y'all.
Make a friend if you can.
Every day people are waking up
To the new one another;
We're on our way,
Making the world a better place.

Three Times:
Reach out, touch a hand.
Make a friend if you can.
Reach out, touch a hand,
Make a friend if you can.

United We Stand

Words and Music by Anthony Toby Hiller and John Goodison

recorded by Brotherhood of Man

There's nowhere in the world that I would rather be
Than with you, my love.
And there's nothing in the world that I would rather see
Than your smile, my love.

Refrain:
For united we stand, divided we fall,
And if our backs should ever be against the wall,
We'll be together, together, you and I.
For united we stand, divided we fall,
And if our backs should ever be against the wall,
We'll be together, together, you and I.

And if the world around you falls apart, my love,
Then I'll still be here.
And if the going gets too hard along the way,
Just you call; I'll hear.

Refrain

Touch Me in the Morning

Words and Music by Ronald Miller and Michael Masser

recorded by Diana Ross

Touch me in the morning,
Then just walk away.
We don't have tomorrow,
But we had yesterday.

(Hey!) Wasn't it me who said that
Nothing good's gonna last forever?
And wasn't it me who said
Let's just be glad for the time together?
Must've been hard to tell me
That you've given all you had to give.
I can understand your feeling that way.
Ev'rybody's got their life to live.

Well, I can say good-bye
In the cold morning light.
But I can't watch love die
In the warmth of the night.
If I've got to be strong,
Don't you know I
Need to have tonight when you're gone?
Till you go I need to lie here and think about
The last time that you'll

Touch me in the morning
Then just close the door.
Leave me as you found me,
Empty like before.

(Hey!) Wasn't it yesterday
We used to laugh at the wind behind us?
Didn't we run away and hope
That time wouldn't try to find us?
Didn't we take each other
To a place where no one's ever been?
Yeah, I really need you near me tonight,
'Cause you'll never take me there again.
Let me watch you go
With the sun in my eyes.
We've seen how love can grow,
Now we'll see how it dies.

If I've got to be strong,
Don't you know I need
To have tonight when you're gone?
Till you go I need to hold you
Until the time your hands reach out and

Duet with Verse 1:
Mornings were blue and gold,
And we could feel one another living.
We walked with a dream to hold,
And we could take what the world was giving.
There's no tomorrow here,
There's only love and the time to chase it.
Yesterday's gone, my love,
There's only now and it's time to face it.

Until It's Time for You to Go

Words and Music by Buffy Sainte-Marie

a standard recorded by various artists

I'm not a dream, I'm not an angel, I'm a man;
You're not a queen, you're a woman, take my hand.
We'll make a space in the lives that we planned.
And here we'll stay until it's time for you to go.

Yes we're different, worlds apart, we're not the same.
We laughed and played at the start like in a game.
You could have stayed outside my heart but in you came.
And here you'll stay until it's time for you to go.

Don't ask why.
Don't ask how.
Don't ask forever.
Love me now!

This love of mine had no beginning, has no end;
I was an oak now I'm a willow now I can bend.
And tho' I'll never in my life see you again.
Still I'll stay until it's time for you to go.

The Way We Were

Words by Alan and Marilyn Bergman
Music by Marvin Hamlisch

from the Motion Picture *The Way We Were*
recorded by Barbra Streisand

Memories
Light the corners of my mind.
Misty, watercolor memories
Of the way we were.

Scattered pictures
Of the smiles we left behind,
Smiles we gave to one another
For the way we were.

Can it be that it was all so simple then,
Or has time rewritten every line?
If we had the chance to do it all again,
Tell me would we? Could we?

Memories
May be beautiful, and yet,
What's too painful to remember
We simply choose to forget.

So it's the laughter
We will remember,
Whenever we remember
The way we were,
The way we were.

Vincent (Starry Starry Night)

Words and Music by Don McLean

recorded by Don McLean

Starry, starry night,
Paint your palette blue and grey.
Look out on a summer's day,
With eyes that know the darkness in my soul.

Shadows on the hills,
Sketch the trees and the daffodils.
Catch the breeze and the winter chills,
In colors on the snowy linen land.

Now I understand
What you tried to say to me,
How you suffered for your sanity,
How you tried to set them free.
They would not listen, they did not know how,
Perhaps they'll listen now.

Starry, starry night,
Flaming flow'rs that brightly blaze.
Swirling clouds in violet haze
Reflect in Vincent's eyes of China blue.

Colors changing hue,
Morning fields of amber grain,
Weathered faces lined in pain,
Are soothed beneath the artist's loving hand.

Now I understand
What you tried to say to me,
How you suffered for your sanity,
How you tried to set them free.
They would not listen they did not know how,
Perhaps they'll listen now.

For they could not love you.
But still your love was true,
And when no hope was left in sight
On that starry, starry night,
You took your life, as lovers often do.
But I could have told you, Vincent,
This world was never meant for one as beautiful as you.

Starry, starry night,
Portraits hung in empty halls.
Frameless heads on nameless walls,
With eyes that watch the world and can't forget.

Like the strangers that you've met,
The ragged men in ragged clothes,
The silver thorn of bloody rose,
Lie crushed and broken on the virgin snow.

Now I think I know
What you tried to say to me,
How you suffered for your sanity,
How you tried to set them free.
They would not listen, they're not list'ning still.
Perhaps they never will.

We Are Family

Words and Music by Nile Rodgers and Bernard Edwards

recorded by Sister Sledge

Refrain:
We are family.
I got all my sisters with me.
We are family.
Get up, everybody and sing.

Everyone can see we're together as we walk on by.
And we flock just like birds of a feather.
I won't tell no lie.
All of the people around u, they say,
"Can they be that close?"
Just let me state for the record:
We're givin' love in a family dose.

Refrain

Living life is fun, and we've just begun
To get our share of this world's delights.
High hopes we have for the future.
And our goal's in sight.
No, we don't get depressed.
We're what we call our golden rule:
Have faith in you and the things you do.
You won't go wrong.
This is our family jewel.

Refrain

We Are the Champions

Words and Music by Freddie Mercury

recorded by Queen

I've paid my dues, time after time.
I've done my sentence but committed no crime.
And bad mistakes, I've made a few.
I've had my share of sand kicked in my face but I've come through.
And I need to go on, and on, and on, and on.

Refrain:
We are the champions my friend.
And we'll keep on fighting till the end.
We are the champions, we are the champions.
No time for losers, 'cause we are the champions of the world.

I've taken my bows and my curtain calls.
You brought me fame and fortune and ev'rything that goes with it,
    I thank you all.
But it's been no bed of roses, no pleasure cruise.
I consider it a challenge before the whole human race and I ain't
    gonna lose.
And I need to go on, and on, and on, and on.

Refrain Twice

We've Got Tonight

Words and Music by Bob Seger

recorded by Bob Seger

I know it's late. I know you're weary.
I know your plans don't include me.
Still, here we are, both of us lonely,
Longing for shelter from all that we see.
Why should we worry? No one will care, girl.
Look at the stars so far away.

Refrain 1:
We've got tonight.
Who needs tomorrow?
We've got tonight babe.
Why don't you stay.

Deep in my soul I've been so lonely.
All of my hopes fading away.
I've longed for love like ev'ryone else does.
I know I'll keep searching even after today.
So there it is, girl. I've said it all now.
And here we are, babe. What do you say?

Refrain 1

I know it's late. I know you're weary.
I know your plans don't include me.
Still, here we are, both of us lonely,
Both of us lonely.

Refrain 2:
We've got tonight. Who needs tomorrow?
Let's make it last. Let's find a way.
Turn out the light. Come take my hand now.
We've got tonight, babe. Why don't you stay?

Refrain 2 Twice

Oh, oh, why don't you stay?

We've Only Just Begun

Words and Music by Roger Nichols and Paul Williams

recorded by Carpenters

We've only just begun to live,
White lace and promises,
A kiss for luck and we're on our way.

Before the rising sun we fly,
So many roads to choose,
We start out walking and learn to run.

Refrain:
And yes, we've just begun.
Sharing horizons that are new to us,
Watching the signs along the way.
Talking it over just the two of us,
Working together day to day, together.

And when the evening comes we smile,
So much of life ahead,
We'll find a place where there's room to grow.

Refrain

And when the evening comes we smile,
So much of life ahead,
We'll find a place where there's room to grow.

And yes, we've just begun.

When I Need You

Words by Carole Bayer Sager
Music by Albert Hammond

recorded by Leo Sayer

When I need you,
I just close my eyes and I'm with you,
And all that I so want to give you,
It's only a heartbeat away.

When I need love,
I hold out my hands and I touch love,
I never knew there was so much love
Keeping me warm night and day.

Miles and miles of empty space in between us,
A telephone can't take the place of your smile.
But you know I won't be traveling forever.
It's cold out, but hold out and do like I do.

When I need you,
I just close my eyes and I'm with you,
And all that I so want to give you, babe,
It's only a heartbeat away.

It's not easy when the road is your driver,
Honey, that's a heavy load that we bear.
But you know I won't be traveling a lifetime.
It's cold out, but hold out and do like I do.

When I need you.

When Will I Be Loved

Words and Music by Phil Everly

recorded by Linda Ronstadt

I've been cheated,
Been mistreated;
When will I be loved?

I've been pushed down,
I've been pushed 'round;
When will I be loved?

When I find my new man
That I want for mine,
He always breaks my heart in two;
It happens every time.

I've been made blue,
I've been lied to;
When will I be loved?

When I find my new man
That I want for mine,
He always breaks my heart in two;
It happens every time.

I've been cheated,
Been mistreated;
When will I be loved?
When will I be loved?
Tell me, when will I be loved?

Where Do I Begin
(Love Theme)

Words by Carl Sigman
Music by Francis Lai

from the Paramount Picture *Love Story*
recorded by Andy Williams

Where do I begin,
To tell the story of how great a love can be,
The sweet love story that is older than the sea,
The simple truth about the love she brings to me?
Where do I start?

With her first hello,
She gave a meaning to this empty world of mine;
There'll never be another love, another time;
She came into my life and made the living fine.
She fills my heart.

She fills my heart with very special things,
With angel songs, with wild imaginings,
She fills my soul with so much love
That anywhere I go I'm never lonely.
With her along, who could be lonely?
I reach for her hand, it's always there.

How long does it last?
Can love be measured by the hours in a day?
I have no answers now, but this much I can say:
I know I'll need her 'til the stars all burn away
And she'll be there.

Where Is the Love?

Words and Music by Ralph MacDonald and William Salter

recorded by Roberta Flack and Donny Hathaway

Where is the love you said you'd give to me
Soon as you were free?
Will it ever be?
Where is the love?

You told me that you didn't love him,
And you were gonna say goodbye.
But if you really didn't mean it,
Why did you have to lie?

Where is the love you said was mine, all mine
Till the end of time?
Was it just a lie?
Where is the love?

If you had a sudden change of heart,
I wish that you would tell me so.
Don't leave me hanging on to promises.
You've got to let me know.

Do do do do…

Oh, how I wish I'd never met you.
I guess it must have been my fate
To fall in love with someone else's love.
All I can do is wait.
That's all I can do, yeah, yeah, yeah.

Repeat and Fade:
Where is the love? Where is the love?
Where is the love? Where is the love?

Why Can't We Be Friends

Words and Music by Sylvester Allen, Harold R. Brown, Morris Dickerson,
Lonnie Jordan, Charles W. Miller, Lee Oskar, Howard Scott and Jerry Goldstein

recorded by War

Ooh, ooh, ooh. Ooh, ooh, ooh,
Ooh, ooh, ooh. Ooh, ooh, ooh.
La la la la la la,
La la la la la la.

Refrain:
Why can't we be friends?
Why can't we be friends?
Why can't we be friends?
Why can't we be friends?

I've seen you around for a long, long time,
I remembered you when you drank my wine.

Refrain

I see you walkin' down in Chinatown,
I called you but you could not turn around.

Refrain

I paid my money to the welfare line,
I see you standin' in it all the time.

Refrain

The color of your skin don't matter to me,
As long as I can live in harmony.

Refrain

I'd kinda like to be the president.
So I can show you how your money's spent.

Refrain

Sometimes I don't speak right,
But yet I know what I'm talking about.

Refrain

I know you're working for the CIA.
They wouldn't have you in the Mafia.

Refrain

Why Me? (Why Me, Lord?)

Words and Music by Kris Kristofferson

recorded by Kris Kristofferson

Why me, Lord?
What have I ever done
To deserve even one of the pleasures I've known?
Tell me, Lord, what did I ever do
That was worth lovin' you or the kindness you've shown?

Refrain:
Lord, help me, Jesus, I've wasted it so.
Help me, Jesus, I know what I am.
But now that I know that I've needed you so,
Help me, Jesus, my soul's in your hand.

Try me, Lord, if you think there's a way
I can try to repay all I've taken from you.
Maybe, Lord, I can show someone else
What I've been through myself on my way back to you.

Refrain Twice

Jesus, my soul's in your hand.

Will It Go Round in Circles

Words and Music by Billy Preston and Bruce Fisher

recorded by Billy Preston

I've got a song I ain't got no melody,
How'm I gonna sing it to my friends?
I've got a song I ain't got no melody,
How'm I gonna sing it to my friends?

Refrain:
Will it go 'round in circles?
Will it fly high like a bird up in the sky?
Will it go 'round in circles?
Will it fly high like a bird up in the sky?

Refrain

I've got a lil' story ain't got no moral,
Let the bad guy win every once in a while.
I've got a story ain't got no moral,
Let the bad guy win every once in a while.

Refrain

I've got a lil' dance ain't got no steps,
I'm gonna let the music move me around.
I've got a dance I ain't got no steps,
I'm gonna let the music move me around.

Repeat Verse 1

Repeat

With a Little Help from My Friends

Words and Music by John Lennon and Paul McCartney

recorded by Joe Cocker, The Beatles

What would you do if sang out of tune,
Would you stand up and walk out on me?
Lend me your ears and I'll play you a song,
And I'll try not to sing out of key.

Refrain:
Oh, I get by with a little help from my friends.
I get high with a little help from my friends.
I'm gonna try with a little help from my friends.

What do I do when my love is away?
(Does it worry you to be alone.)
How do I feel by the end of the day?
(Are you sad because you're on your own.)

Refrain

Bridge:
Do you need anybody?
I need somebody to love.
Could it be anybody?
I want somebody to love.

Would you believe in a love at first sight?
Yes, I'm certain that it happens all the time.
What do you see when you turn out the light?
I can't tell you but I know it's mine. Oh,

Repeat Refrain, Bridge and Refrain

Yes, I get by with a little help from my friends.

The Wonder of You

Words and Music by Baker Knight

recorded by Elvis Presley

When no one else can understand me,
When ev'rything I do is wrong,
You give me love and consolation.
You give me hope to carry on,
And you try to show your love for me in ev'rything you do.
That's the wonder, the wonder of you.

And when you smile, the world is brighter.
You touch my hand and I'm a king.
Your kiss to me is worth a fortune.
Your love to me is ev'rything,
And you're always there to lend a hand in all I try to do.
That's the wonder, the wonder of you.

You'll never know how much I love you.
My love is yours and yours alone,
And it's so wonderful to have you.
To have you for my very own.
Guess I'll never know the reason why you love me as you do.
That's the wonder, the wonder of you.

Yesterday Once More

Words and Music by John Bettis and Richard Carpenter

recorded by Carpenters

When I was young I'd listen to the radio
Waitin' for my favorite songs
When they played I'd sing along; it made me smile.
Those were such happy times and not so long ago,
How I wondered where they'd gone.
But they're back again just like a long lost friend,
All the songs I love so well.

Refrain:
Every sha-la-la-la, every wo, wo, wo still shines.
Every shinga-ling-a-ling that they're startin' to sing so fine.

When they get to the part where he's breaking her heart
It can really make me cry just like before.
It's yesterday once more. (Shoobie do lang lang.)

Lookin' back on how it was in years gone by
And the good times that I had,
Makes today seem rather sad, so much has changed.
It was songs of love that I would sing to then.
And I'd memorize each word.
Those old melodies still sound so good to me,
As they melt the years away.

Refrain

All my best memories come back clearly to me,
Some can even make me cry just like before.

Refrain

Y.M.C.A.

Words and Music by Jacques Morali, Henri Belolo and Victor Willis

recorded by Village People

Young man, there's no need to feel down.
I said, young man, pick yourself off the ground.
I said, young man, 'cause you're in a new town
There's no need to be unhappy.

Young man, there's a place you can go,
I said, young man, when you're short on your dough.
You can stay there and I'm sure you will find
Many ways to have a good time.

It's fun to stay at the Y.M.C.A.
It's fun to stay at the Y.M.C.A.
They have everything for young men to enjoy.
You can hang out with all the boys.

It's fun to stay at the Y.M.C.A.
It's fun to stay at the Y.M.C.A.
You can get yourself clean, you can have a good meal.
You can do whatever you feel.

Young man, are you listening to me?
I said, young man what do you want to be?
I said, young man you can make real your dreams
But you've got to know this one thing.

No man does it all by himself.
I said young man put your pride on the shelf.
And just go there to the Y.M.C.A.
I'm sure they can help you today.

It's fun to stay at the Y.M.C.A.
It's fun to stay at the Y.M.C.A.
They have everything for young men to enjoy.
You can hang out with all the boys.

It's fun to stay at the Y.M.C.A.
It's fun to stay at the Y.M.C.A.
Young man, young man, there's no need to feel down.
Young man, young man, pick yourself off the ground.

Young man, I was once in your shoes
I said, I was down and out and with the blues.
I felt no man cared if I were alive.
I felt the whole world was so jive.

That's when someone come up to me
And said, "Young man, take a walk up the street.
It's a place there called the Y.M.C.A.
They can start you back on your way."

It's fun to stay at the Y.M.C.A.
It's fun to stay at the Y.M.C.A.
They have everything for young men to enjoy.
You can hang out with all the boys.

It's fun to stay at the Y.M.C.A.
It's fun to stay at the Y.M.C.A.
Young man, young man, are you listening to me?
Young man, young man, what do you want to be?

Repeat and Fade:
Y.M.C.A.
It's fun to stay at the Y.M.C.A.
They have everything for young men to enjoy.
You can hang out with all the boys.

You and Me Against the World

Words and Music by Paul Williams and Ken Ascher

recorded by Helen Reddy

You and me against the world.
Sometimes it feels like you and me against the world.
When all others turn their back and walk away,
You can count on me to stay.
Remember when the circus came to town,
And you were frightened by the clown?
Wasn't it nice to be around someone that you knew,
Someone who was big and strong,
And lookin' out for you and me against the world.

And for all the times we've cried,
I always felt the odds were on our side.
And when one of us is gone,
And one is left alone to carry on,
Well, then remembering will have to do.
Our memories alone will get us through.
Think about the days of me and you,
Of you and me against the world.

Life can be a circus.
They under pay and over work us,
And though we seldom get our due,
When each day is through,
I bring my tired body home,
And look around for me and you against the world.
Sometimes it feels like you and me against the world.

And for all the times we've cried,
I always felt that God was on our side.
And when one of us is gone,
And one is left alone to carry on,
Well, then remembering will have to do.
Our memories alone will get us through.
Think about the days of me and you,
Of you and me against the world.

You Are So Beautiful

Words and Music by Billy Preston and Bruce Fisher

recorded by Joe Cocker

You are so beautiful to me.
You are so beautiful to me.
Can't you see you're everything that I hope for
And what's more, you're everything I need.
You are so beautiful, baby, to me.

You're everything that I hope for
And what's more, you're everything I need.
You are so beautiful, baby, to me.

Such joy and happiness you bring.
(I wanna thank you babe.)
Such joy and happiness you bring,
Just like a dream.
You're the guiding light shinin' in the night,
You're heaven still to me.
(Hey baby,)

You are so beautiful.
You are so beautiful.

You Are the Sunshine of My Life

Words and Music by Stevie Wonder

recorded by Stevie Wonder

You are the sunshine of my life,
That's why I'll always be around.
You are the apple of my eye.
Forever you'll stay in my heart.

I feel like this is the beginning,
'Though I've loved you for a million years.
And if I thought our love was ending,
I'd find myself, drowning in my own tears.

You are the sunshine of my life,
That's why I'll always stay around.
You are the apple of my eye.
Forever you'll stay in my heart.

You must have known that I was lonely,
Because you came to my rescue.
And I know that this must be heaven;
How could so much love, be inside of you?

Repeat Verse 1 and Fade

You Belong to Me

Words and Music by Carly Simon and Michael McDonald

recorded by Carly Simon

Why'd you tell me this?
Were you looking for my reaction?
What do you need to know?
Don't you know I'll always be your girl?

Refrain:
You don't have to prove to me
You're beautiful to strangers.
I've got loving eyes of my own. (You belong to me.)
Tell her you were fooling. (You belong to me.)
You don't even know her. (You belong to me.)
Tell her that I love you. (You belong to me.)

You belong to me.
Can it be that you're not sure?
You belong to me.
Thought we'd closed the book; locked the door.

Refrain

You Decorated My Life

Words and Music by Debbie Hupp and Bob Morrison

recorded by Kenny Rogers

All my life was a paper,
Once plain, pure, and white,
Till you moved with your pen,
Changin' moods now and then
Till the balance was right.
Then you added some music,
Ev'ry note was in place;
And anybody could see all the changes in me
By the look on my face.

Refrain:
And you decorated my life,
Created a world where dreams are a part.
And you decorated my life
By paintin' your love all over my heart.
You decorated my life.

Like a rhyme with no reason
In an unfinished song,
There was no harmony,
Life meant nothin' to me
Until you came along.
And you brought out the colors,
What a gentle surprise;
Now I'm able to see all the things life can be,
Shinin' soft in your eyes.

Refrain

You Don't Bring Me Flowers

Words by Neil Diamond, Marilyn Bergman and Alan Bergman
Music by Neil Diamond

recorded by Neil Diamond & Barbra Streisand

You don't bring me flowers
You don't sing me love songs
You hardly talk to me anymore
When you come through the door
At the end of the day

I remember when
You couldn't wait to love me
Used to hate to leave me
Now after lovin' me late at night
When it's good for you
And you're feelin' alright,
Well you just roll over
And you turn out the light
And you don't bring me flowers anymore

It used to be so natural
To talk about forever
But used to be's don't count anymore
They just lay on the floor
'Til we sweep them away

And baby, I remember
All the things you taught me
I learned how to laugh
And I learned how to cry
Well I learned how to love
Even learned how to lie
You'd think I could learn
How to tell you goodbye
'Cause you don't bring me flowers anymore

You Don't Have to Be a Star (To Be in My Show)

Words and Music by John Glover and James Dean

recorded by Marilyn McCoo and Billy Davis, Jr.

Male: Baby, come as you are
With just your heart, and I'll take you in.
You're rejected and hurt;
To me you're worth what you have within.

Female: Now I don't need no superstar,
'Cause I'll accept you as you are.
You won't be denied, 'cause I'm satisfied
With the love you inspire.

Male: You don't have to be a star, baby,
To be in my show.
Female: You don't have to be a star, baby,
To be in my show.

Male: Somebody nobody knows
Could steal the tune that you wanna hear.
So stop your runnin' around,
'Cause now you've found
What was cloudy is clear. Oh honey.

Female: There'll be no cheering from the crowds,
Male: Just two hearts beating out loud.
Female: There'll be no parades, no T.V. or stage,
Only me till your dying day.

Both: You don't have to be a star, baby,
To be in my show.
You don't have to be a star, baby,
To be in my, my, my, my, my, my show.

Male: Don't think your star has to shine
For me to find out where you're coming from.
What is a beauty queen if it don't mean
I'm your number one? Oh, honey.

And I don't need no superstar,
'Cause I'll accept you as you are.
You won't be denied, 'cause I'm satisfied
With the love you inspire

Both: You don't have to be a star, baby,
To be in my show.
You don't have to be a star, baby,
To be in my show.

You Light Up My Life

Words and Music by Joseph Brooks

recorded by Debby Boone

So many nights I'd sit by my window
Waiting for someone to sing me his song.
So may dreams I kept deep inside me,
Alone in the dark, but now you've come along.

Refrain:
And you light up my life.
You give me hope to carry on.
You light up my days
And fill my nights with song.

Rollin' at sea, adrift on the waters,
Could it be finally I'm turning for home?
Finally a chance to say, "Hey! I love you."
Never again to be all alone.

Refrain Twice

It can't be wrong when it feels so right,
'Cause you, you light up my life.

You Needed Me

Words and Music by Randy Goodrum

recorded by Anne Murray

I cried a tear, you wiped it dry.
I was confused, you cleared my mind.
I sold my soul, you bought it back for me
And held me up and gave me dignity.
Somehow you needed me.

Refrain:
You gave me strength to stand alone again
To face the world out on my own again
You put me high upon a pedestal
So high that I can almost see eternity.
You needed me. You needed me.

And I can't believe it's you, I can't believe it's true.
I needed you and you were there
And I'll never leave. Why should I leave?
I'd be a fool
'Cause I've finally found someone
Who really cares.

You held my hand when it was cold.
When I was lost, you took me home.
You gave me hope, when I was at the end,
And turned my lies back into truth again.
You even called me friend.

Refrain

You Make Me Feel Like Dancing

Words and Music by Vini Poncia and Leo Sayer

recorded by Leo Sayer

You've got a cute way of talking;
You got the better of me.
Just snap your fingers and I'm walking like a dog,
Hanging on your lead.
I'm in a spin, you know;
Shaking on a string, you know.

Refrain:
You make me feel like dancing;
I wanna dance the night away.
You make me feel like dancing;
I'm gonna dance the night away.
You make me feel like dancing.
I feel like dancing, dancing, dance the night away.
I feel like dancing, dancing.

Quarter to four in the morning,
I ain't feeling tired, no. no. no.
Just hold me tight and leave on the light,
'Cause I don't wanna go home.
You put a spell on me;
I'm right where you want me to be.

Refrain

Dance the night away.
I feel like dancing, dancing, dance the night away.
I feel like dancing, dancing, ah.

And if you'll let me stay, we'll dance our lives away.

Repeat and Fade:
You make me feel like dancing;
I wanna dance my life way.
You make me fell like dancing;
I wanna dance my life away.

You Sexy Thing

Words and Music by E. Brown

recorded by Hot Chocolate

Refrain:
I believe in miracles.
Where you from, you sexy thing?
I believe in miracles
Since you came along, you sexy thing.

Where did you come from, baby?
How did you know I needed you?
How did you know I needed you so badly?
How did you know I'd give my heart gladly?
Yesterday I was one of the lonely people.
Now you're lying close to me, makin' love to me.

Refrain

Where did you come from, angel?
How did you know I'd be the one?
Did you know you're everything I prayed for?
Did you know? Every night and day,
For every day, givin' love and satisfaction.
Now you're lying next to me, givin' it to me.

Refrain

Kiss me, you sexy thing.
Touch me, baby, you sexy thing.
I love the way you touch me darling, you sexy thing.
You sexy, you sexy thing.
Yesterday I was one of the lonely people.
Now you're lying close to me, givin' it to me.

Refrain

Touch me, you sexy thing.
Touch me, baby, you sexy thing.
I love the way you hold me, baby, you sexy thing.
You sexy, you sexy thing. You sexy thing.

You're in My Heart

Words and Music by Rod Stewart

recorded by Rod Stewart

I didn't know what day it was
When you walked into the room.
I said hello. I noticed
You said good-bye too soon.

Breezin' through the clientele,
Spinning yarns that were so lyrical.
I really must confess right here,
The attraction was purely physical.

I took all those habits of yours
That in the beginning were hard to accept.
Your fashion sense, Beardsly prints,
I put down to experience.

The big-bosomed lady with the Dutch accent
Who tried to change my point of view.
Her ad-libbed lines were well rehearsed,
But my heart cried out for you.

Refrain:
You're in my heart.
You're in my soul.
You'll be my breath should I grow old.
You are my lover, you're my best friend.
You're in my soul.

My love for you is immeasurable,
My respect for you immense.
You're ageless, timeless, lace and fineness.
You're beauty and elegance.

You're a rhapsody, a comedy.
You're a symphony and a play.
You're ev'ry love song ever written,
But honey, what do you see in me?

Refrain

You're an essay in glamor.
Please pardon the grammar,
But you're ev'ry schoolboy's dream.
You're Celtic united, but baby I've decided
You're the best team I've ever seen.

And there have been many affairs
And many times I've thought to leave.
But I bite my lip and turn around,
'Cause you're the warmest thing I've ever found.

Refrain

You're My Best Friend

Words and Music by John Deacon

recorded by Queen

Ooh, you make me live;
Whatever this world can give to me.
It's you, you're all I see.
Ooh, you make me live now, honey,
Ooh, you make me live.

Ooh, you're the best friend that I ever had.
I've been with you such a long time,
You're my sunshine and I want you to know,
That my feelings are true,
I really love you.

Refrain:
Oh, you're my best friend.
Ooh, you make me live.
Ooh, I've been wandering 'round,
But I still come back to you.
In rain or shine you've stood by me, girl.
I'm happy at home,
You're my best friend.

Ooh, you make me live
Whenever this world is cruel to me.
I got you to help me forgive.
Ooh, you make me live now, honey,
Ooh, you make me live.

Ooh, you're the first one when things turn out bad.
You know I'll never be lonely,
You're my only one and I love the things,
I really love the things that you do.

Refrain

Ooh, ooh, you're my best friend.
Ooh, you make me live.
Ooh, you're my best friend.

You're So Vain

Words and Music by Carly Simon

recorded by Carly Simon

You walked into the party like you were walking onto a yacht;
Your hat strategically dipped below one eye, your scarf, it was apricot.
You had one eye in the mirror as you watched yourself gavotte
And all the girls dreamed that they'd be your partner, they'd be your
    partner and

Refrain:
You're so vain,
You probably think this song is about you,
You're so vain.
I bet you think this song is about you.
Don't you? Don't you?

You had me several years ago when I was still quite naive;
Well, you said that we made such a pretty pair, and that you would
    never leave.
But you gave away the things you loved and one of them was me.
I had some dreams, they were clouds in my coffee, clouds in my coffee
    and

Refrain

Well, I hear you went up to Saratoga, and your horse naturally won;
Then, you flew your Lear jet up to Nova Scotia, to see the total eclipse
    of the sun.
Well, you're where you should be all the time and when you're not
    you're with
Some underworld spy or the wife of a close friend, wife of a close
    friend and

Refrain

Repeat and Fade:
You're so vain, you probably think this song is about you.

You've Got a Friend

Words and Music by Carole King

recorded by James Taylor

When you're down and troubled,
And you need some loving care;
(or: And you need a helping hand;)
And nothin' is goin' right
Close your eyes and think of me,
And soon I will be there
To brighten up even your darkest night.

You just call out my name,
And you know wherever I am
I'll come runnin' to see you again.
Winter, spring, summer or fall,
All you have to do is call,
And I'll be there.
You've got a friend.

If the sky above you
Grows dark and full of clouds;
And that old north wind begins to blow
Keep your head together,
And call my name out loud;
Soon you'll hear me knockin' at your door.

You just call out my name,
And you know wherever I am
I'll come runnin' to see you again.
Winter, spring, summer or fall,
All you have to do is call,
And I'll be there, yes, I will.

Now ain't it good to know that you've got a friend,
When people can be so cold?
They'll hurt you,
Yes, and desert you,
And take your soul, if you let them.
Oh, but don't you let them.

You just call out my name,
And you know wherever I am
I'll come runnin' to see you a gain.
Winter, spring, summer or fall,
All you have to do is call,
And I'll be there, yes, I will.

You've got a friend.
You've got a friend.
Ain't it good to know
You've got a friend...

Your Song

Words and Music by Elton John and Bernie Taupin

recorded by Elton John

It's a little bit funny this feeling inside,
I'm not one of those who can easily hide,
I don't have much money, but, if I did,
I'd buy a big house where we both could live.

If I were a sculptor but then again no,
Or a man who makes potions in a travelin' show,
I know it's not much but it's the best I can do,
My gift is my song and this one's for you.

Refrain:
And you can tell ev'rybody this is your song.
It may be quite simple but, now that it's done,
I hope you don't mind, I hope you don't mind
That I put down in words,
How wonderful life is while you're in the world.

I sat on the roof and kicked off the moss,
Well a few of the verses, well they've got me quite cross,
But the sun's been quite kind while I wrote this song.
It's for people like you that keep it turned on.

So excuse me forgetting but these things I do,
You see I've forgotten if they're green or they're blue,
Anyway the thing is what I really mean,
Yours are the sweetest eyes I've ever seen.

Refrain

I hope you don't mind, I hope you don't mind
That I put down in words,
How wonderful life is while you're in the world.